LITTLE CHANGES

TALES OF A *Reluctant* HOME ECO-MOMICS PIONEER

KRISTI MARSH

IN COLLABORATION WITH RACHEL VIDONI

ORIGINAL ILLUSTRATIONS BY KATHRYN TEMPESTOSO

lil' red

cardinal

This book is available for purchase at www.choosewiser.com, www.Amazon.com, and at selected bookstores. Audio book, eBook, and book club volume discounts are available at www.choosewiser.com or at (508) 364-2649.

For information about bringing the author to your live event, contact Choose Wiser at (508) 364-2649, or email info@Choosewiser.com.

Original illustrations and cover art by Kathryn Tempestoso.

Published by Lil' Red Cardinal. Printed and bound in the United States.

This publication contains the opinions and ideas of its author. It is intended to provide helpful and informative material on the subjects addressed in the publication. It is sold with the understanding that the author and publisher are not engaged in rendering medical, health, psychological, or any other kind of personal or professional services in the book.

The author and publisher specifically disclaim all responsibility for any liability, loss, or risk, personal or otherwise, that is incurred as a consequence, directly or indirectly from the use and application of any of the contents of this book.

Library of Congress 2011944321

First Edition

ISBN 0984009647 (pbk.)

ISBN 13: 9780984009640

To my Buggy, Wylie Woo, and Princess Pie.

For giving me a job to do.

To my infant nephew, Philip.

May you grow up to find my story laughable and the journey obsolete.

D

Contents

Next

Saliva seeped into the hollows under my tongue, preparing my body for the first wave of nausea. I closed my eyes and clutched the car door handle. My upper lip quivering, I exhaled a barely audible moan. I murmured to my husband, "Hon, I think…I think I'm feeling ill. It feels…like I'm seasick." He said nothing, but I felt his presence stiffen with the protective mission to transport me home. The commute from the inner corridors of Boston to the suburbs was notorious for sluggish traffic. To quicken our drive, I disappeared inside my head.

With closed eyes, I lifted my feet onto the dashboard and slumped down into my seat searching my memory. *Was this queasiness similar to my morning sickness? What had that been like?* My first pregnancy was just eight years ago, but I was having a hard time concentrating. I scanned my memory files again. Ah, yes. I had mild, not remarkable, morning sickness with my pregnancies. Our towhead boys, Tanner and Kyle, were eight and six, and my baby girl Kaytee had just left her fierce threes. My life was full, loud, active, and deeply gratifying. My soul smiled, longing for my three anxious children. Perhaps this nausea, this poison, wasn't so bad.

After my tumor removal surgery a month before, the doctors informed me that chances were good the cancer was gone. But a chance is a chance, not a guarantee. The stakes were too high to leave even one cell floating in my body. One rogue microscopic cell swirling in my system could lead to the unimaginable. I understood. I would undergo chemotherapy.

Earlier that day, my husband escorted me to the world renowned Dana Farber Cancer Institute in Boston. Shoulders back. Chin up. I walked down the soothingly decorated hospital hallway. As I advanced past curtain-drawn cubicles, I caught glimpses of dispirited, elderly patients hooked up to plastic piping. Alone, I had to sit my body down in the oversized vinyl chair in the midst of sterile alcohol fumes. There was no space in my mind for self-pity. Or for being scared. A fierceness rose from a depth I didn't know existed. With a warrior's vengeance, I internally snarled, *How dare cancer enter my life!* The oncology nurse, wisely knowing what my afternoon held, slid on protective gloves and hooked tubing to my recently implanted chest plug.

Arriving home, my husband ushered me upstairs to the bedroom. I curled into a fetal position in the darkness, preparing for combat. It had been four hours since merciless, bounty-hunter poisons—Adriamycin and its accomplice Cytoxan—were dripped into my body to annihilate cancer cells, but time seemed irrelevant. I visualized the poisons snaking through miles of veins. Down my arm, up and down each finger, cascading through arteries in my leg, and returning to my core. Venom-blood rivers rushing to decimate the cancer and with it, innocent bystander tissues. My stomach lining. The roof of my mouth. The cells that produce hair. Circulating. Eradicating.

My physical body revolted against the foreign liquids in its veins. Protectively, it initiated a system-wide shut down of my senses. Soft rumbling from the clothes dryer one floor below caused me to whimper. The image of tumbling, rolling clothes exacerbated the nausea. Blue, flickering television light from the family room outside my door made me cringe. I brought my fist up to my forehead and sheltered my eyes in the blackness. As my soul witnessed the fighting inside, I thankfully sensed warm tears slide across my cheekbones. They assured me I was still part of this world.

I escaped by disappearing deep into memories—to a rocky cove and a sandy beach. The sun was melting into a pink celebration at dusk. Low tide revealed dark rocks filled with creeping crustaceans. My children, with wind-whipped hair and marshmallow-golden sun-kissed shoulders, collected ocean specimens in colored plastic pail aquariums. This was *my* happy place. Not even an arsenal of poison could eradicate this peace.

For me, this marked the beginning of my fight against the all too-common breast cancer. I had read one in eight women in the United States would be diagnosed. I prayed I was taking one for the team so that my friends and daughter would ride safely in my statistic and never become initiated into this sorority. I could hardly bear to think of loved ones enduring the slash and burn of operations and chemotherapy. Still, as brutal as modern methods may be, these chemicals have a place in our society. I am deeply appreciative for the science, drugs, and toxins that came to my defense. They gave me life.

They gave me today.

In the aftermath of chemotherapy, I was thrust into an enthralling predicament. A do-over. I could resume with the comfortably familiar, or I could redefine my interpretations of living a healthy life. I could do what I had always done, or I could challenge my standards in search of a new and different outlook. Neither choice revealed a timeline; neither was wrong. Tentative, yet trusting, I chose the latter and embarked on a life foreign to my family's experiences. I gutted our routines and started to rebuild, not only my body, but also our rituals and expectations. Most decisions were exhilarating, infused with a delightful buzz. Yet some days, gut-wrenching revelations dropped me to my knees, and I pleaded to return to virgin days of ignorance. But knowledge prevents retreat, and I could not go back. I gripped my children's paws and pulled them close. Five years later, with incredible purpose, I can say nothing has ever felt more right. This was and is *living*.

My movements rippled and resonated in the curious. Friends followed their own passions, entertained by my modifications to mainstream motherhood. Eventually, national media celebrated my actions, my way of living. Yet, I am not alone. It was just my turn. My story is not about trudging through cancer's dreary and devastating wake.

It's about what happened next.

New Dawn

Birds flying high.
You know how I feel.
Sun in the sky.
You know how I feel.
Breeze driftin' on by.
You know how I feel.

It's a new dawn
It's a new day
It's a new life
For me....

And I'm feeling' good.

~ written by Anthony Newley
and Leslie Bricusse

A New Job Description

Before finding the lump during a quick shower on a ski trip, I was a list makin', event organizin', club leadin', stay-at-home mom. I was acclimating to the rotation of morning preschool, afternoon kindergarten, and third grade activities, when everything changed. In the moments between "You have cancer" and the soft thud of the phone on the maple dresser, my life took on new meaning. Every cell, every nucleus in my body aligned with primal intent: survive to be a mother to my children. During these moments, I did not feel fear. I felt fierce. Protective. Pissed. *If this is what I have to deal with, then bring it.* Nothing, NOTHING, was going to take my job from me.

The surgeon performing my mastectomy was disheartened to discover not just the lump in question but also, sprawling against my chest wall, a disc-like tumor the diameter of a Reese's Peanut Butter Cup. It had methodically crept into my right armpit, tainting lymph nodes and maliciously threatening to leave my children motherless. While I was healing from surgery, wrapped in bandages and with drainage tubing tucked under my armpit, experts analyzed slices of the confiscated tumor. The findings categorized my tumor unscientifically as angry and aggressive, solidifying my future as a chemotherapy patient.

Being thirty-six had its pros and cons. The pro? Since I was otherwise healthy, doctors determined I should be able to sustain a pounding. The con however, was that my age statistically left many decades for possible recurrence. Therefore, every modern method was prescribed for my personalized cancer-killing cocktail: six months of chemotherapy, a year of targeted gene therapy infusion, and a thirty-five day radiation marathon. Heart scans, bone scans, MRIs, and blood work seized empty calendar squares. My number had been called; I was drafted into the army of full-time oncology warriors. I was unusually young, but unusually young is quickly becoming not so unusual.

Not in control of my cancer, my treatment, or my outcome, I carefully scratched my to-do list chronologically in black pen. It filled the length of a white, piece of lined binder paper. I held onto my precious checklist like a toddler with a security blanket, tucking it under my arm from one doctor appointment to another. Occasionally at night, I removed it from the right hand desk drawer to calculate, again, how many years this was going to take. With resolve, I engraved each black checkmark. As long as I had my list in my possession, I could inch toward normalcy.

On New Year's Eve 2006, shortly after my first chemo treatment, I laid a white bathroom towel around my shoulders and handed scissors to my children. I encouraged them to have fun cutting my shoulder-length blonde locks into an above-the-ear bob. "The good medicine is doing its job, but it has a SILLY side effect," I told them. "It is going to make my hair fall out. Isn't that crazy?" Chemo stopped the production of hair cells about ten days before the effects would be visible. Maybe I could set a positive tone and prepare them for my imminent physical changes. "Hair is just hair, see? I am still Mommy."

As the chemo went to work, I started to shed like my Labrador, leaving a trail around the house. A week later, in the preschool parking lot, bitter New England winds brushed hair right out of its follicles. I stood there alone, raking my fingers through what was left, releasing clumps into the wind, and watching it disappear into the dreary, barren woods. Before cancer, the thought of scraggly tufts and chicken-skin scalp was mortifying. Now, training as a cancer warrior, I thought differently. Chemotherapy hard at work was my ally, not the evil enemy.

Oddly, we made room for our unexpected poisonous houseguest and nestled into a rhythm. One day of infusion. Several days of destruction. Two weeks of regaining just-enough strength. Check it off. Do it again. During these cycles, I was blessed to have an extensive support posse. Cancer tends to draw family and friends toward you like having a beach house on Nantucket, and I was grateful for the help. Moms whisked my children off to karate lessons and birthday parties. Neighbors tucked foil-wrapped chicken casseroles into a cooler outside the front door. Relatives and dear friends flew thousands of miles, leaving their children to comfort mine. It was a relief to know Tanner, Kyle, and Kaytee's lives were enveloped in love. While they were nurtured, I was spoiled with prayers and encouragement. Girlfriends gathered to throw a Chemo-Shower, complete with Kristi's-life-bingo and gifts of printed scarves and stylish hats. Flowers were delivered in a stream, announced by the doorbell, and displayed around our home like a tropical garden. While the flowers eventually were composted, and the food enjoyed, I stored the avalanche of Hallmark cards on my closet shelf. I admit that, occasionally, I resented sympathy cards expressing deep sorrow. I felt they implied that something other than surviving was in my future. Other tidings were sent purposefully to elicit a smile, filled with rah-rah handwritten notes or with photos of naughty half-naked muscular models on the front. They worked. I smiled. In a life of e-everything, whimsical and humorous cards brought laughter to the gravity.

While many memories are foggy, distinct cravings are vivid. Grandma Marsh shipped buckets of Wyoming-made Chex mix—salty, buttery, and crunchy—satisfying the demand for protein and carbs. Papa Terry shipped Leatherby's banana walnut ice cream from California to my New England doorstep. My desire for ice cream is lifelong, not medicinal, but the unorthodox gesture was heavenly. Above all, I craved and longed desperately to be plain ol' me. I wanted my mundane life back, the one unworthy of swirly-italic fonted cards. This yearning incited brazen behavior, and I ignored caution to isolate myself from germ-infested crowds. One Saturday, we piled kids and hot cocoa into the SUV to skate at the nearby pond-turned-rink. Bundled and laced up, I took my daughter's mittened hand to counterbalance her choppy, Frankenstein-like first-time skating moves. Round and round we went in the icy air, and no one knew it was me. Decked out in winter clothing, I blended into the crowd. No one felt uncomfortable or sorrowful in my presence. No one felt awkward about what to ask or not ask. I was doing what I was supposed to be doing. My job. I tipped my chin sun-ward and soaked in the moment.

I didn't even know a photographer had captured the scene until the following Friday, when the town paper celebrated the sunny winter break with a sepia photo of an unnamed mother and daughter. Readers didn't know the two auburn braids was a wig, secured into place with a knit ski hat. They didn't know the oversized sunglasses did more than protect against the snow's sunny glare; they hid dark circles. In this picture perfect slice of time, I was just a mom. Carefully, I pinned my

beloved clipping to my feel-good corkboard, my paper-thin proof I was triumphant. It hung on display among magazine clippings of a Jaguar convertible and an advertisement for a glowing log cabin as well as many random pictures of my children. When I needed comforting, I traced the photos with my finger, pretending that if my life were ever movie-worthy, I would already have the opening scene scripted. It would show a faded newspaper clipping fluttering to the floor in slow motion with a close-up of this arbitrary winter scene; an extra-ordinary, Everyday-Me.

Back to work, visualizing a healthy body while lying on my bedroom floor, I ruminated over the healing taking place within me and giggled. I wasn't just rebuilding. This process was giving birth to a new physical body, cell by cell. Delivering life in any form requires labor. After chemo ravaged my body, innate intelligence went to work. New bone cells sifted into place. My lungs trained for the goal of twenty-three-thousand oxygen-cleansing motions a day. A gummy layer of stomach mucus restored its lining. Amazed and helpless, I mothered my body during the days and paced the family room in moonlight like a nervous new father.

Even though unseen miracles were hard at work daily, growing eyebrows stretched over two long months. Who knew those tiny hairs took such energy to produce? The irony is that I spent plenty of time in my former life plucking those suckers out trying to achieve the perfect arc, and here I was cheering on their growth. How many actors receive acclaim when they shave their heads for a cancer patient role? Where is the leading woman who shaved her eyebrows and plucked eyelashes for the complete de-humanizing effect? One morning, leaning three inches from the bathroom mirror and through my breath's fog, I glee-fully spotted sprouting stubble. Infant eyebrows! What a proud mama I made! Their arrival was synchronized with prickly hair pushing out of my scalp. I looked like a sluggish version of my daughter's Play Dough hair salon. More and more, I put aside my blue paisley I-Have-Cancer scarf as peach fuzz formed into a longer fifth grade boy's buzz cut. Even though my hair was making its ascent, it would take months before I removed the eyebrow pencil from my purse. Not only could I fill in my sparse brows, but it also boosted my spirits to shade my hairline, creating an illusion of thick luscious stubble.

In addition to new eyebrows, I was in awe of my tireless body cranking out over a million red blood cells per second. Like worker bees in a swarm, red blood cells picked up packages of oxygen in my lungs and delivered them to tired, depleted tissues. They brought color to my pale facial features and eased the awkward shock for polite visitors. Producing white blood cells was another beloved treasure. The little gems protect against life-threatening infections, bacteria, parasites, and other enemy invaders. They were terribly important as my first line of defense but were notoriously slaughtered by chemotherapy cocktails. My body ramped production goals to an impressive billion white blood cells a day. One billion! If I tried to count to a billion, it would take me thirty-two years. The magnificence of our bodies captivated me.

By the time my third treatment date queued itself on my binder paper, I had a small routine in place. Coordinate the family. Clear the week. Meditate. Slide on stretchy, navy yoga pants. Dig through my husband's drawer for a loose shirt for easy access to the port-a-cath.*
Arriving at the clinic, I ascended five flights of stairs to the oncology floor, insisting that as long as I had "feet on my legs" I would skip the elevators. Conversational banter moved me through registration and routine blood work. As I waited to begin treatment, my favorite nurse delivered a right hook to my gut. "I'm sorry Mrs. Marsh; your white blood count is too low. It is too risky to treat you today. You'll have to go home."

Go home? I'm sorry. Did she just tell a cancer patient to *go home?*

Ms. Nurse politely instructed me to whip up a couple hundred thousand white blood cells before returning to cancer annihilation, as if it were a task I could control. Go home, bake cookies, make leukocytes. Easy peasy. Stunned, I just stood there. I was in the middle of fighting something very important here! What do you mean go home?

---

* The port-a-cath was a contraption embedded under my pectoral tissue and skin. Rubbing my fingers over it, it reminded me of the pop-up button on a Thanksgiving turkey. It was through this portal that the nurse dripped bags of liquids into my veins.

I WANTED my chemo. It was next on my list—see my paper? Raw disbelief morphed into a trembling chin and tears for a chemo delayed. Dark disappointment filled the silent ride home, where I was to continue to build, heal, and nurture my body.

The doctors added an extra week to my to-do list, but really, life was giving me a two-year time-out. As much as I wanted to rejoin chaos, this pause was an aberrant gift. Instead of being a slave to multi-tasking and over-scheduled bedlam, I was given room to reflect amidst the quiet. In this silence, my mind acknowledged what my soul understood; our bodies have a singular purpose—an overwhelming obsession to survive and give us the gift of the best life possible. I had little control of what was happening under my own skin, whether it was pumping my heart or replenishing blood cells, but I could choose to languish or flourish. It would be sacrilegious to knowingly compromise my body's intent. Not as a patient. Not as a healthy, loving mom. It was here, wrapped in this understanding, that my life shifted on its axis.

Whether my life offered me one day or forty more glorious years, I suddenly had direction. I wanted my actions to be guided by one priority: health. Cancer would force me to take time off. Fine. I decided to use this gift to plan my future, to figure out how I could encourage a healthier lifestyle for myself and for my family. *But to what extent do my actions influence my physical body? Do I compromise its potential or encourage it?* Sure, I had been a lifelong gym member, loved eating healthfully, dutifully applied sunscreen, and buckled my seatbelt. Evidently, this wasn't enough. Though I couldn't control the fact I had cancer, could I control other influences in my life? Were the products I purchased and used healthy for me? Was the food I provided for my family the best I could find and place on the table? Did the products I used to clean my home keep out the germs or compromise my family's health in some way? Could I fine-tune my choices outside of exercise and a balanced diet? The bottom-line question was: could I influence my health *through* my surroundings? I hoped so. It was becoming evident that without health, I had nothing. I heard the old adage in my head, "You can't know where you're going until you know where you've been." I decided to start there, by reflecting on my past decisions and choices. Where *had* I been exactly? And *why* had I been there?

What Was Really Bugging Me?

As newlyweds, Ted and I had relocated from the glorious blue and emerald Pacific Northwest to the brick and grey of Boston, Massachusetts. We accepted the offer to move back East in 1998 as a three-year career voyage to explore the world. It was an adventure, but I was cautious. My childhood had been infused with riding my horse bareback through golden fields, romancing Pacific coastal beaches, and treasuring the massive Sierra Nevada mountain range. In my mind, the Northeast consisted of polluted, sprawling cities. Wouldn't an area as old as the Mayflower be asphalted and over-populated? Instead, my ignorance was pleasantly replaced with the discovery of quaint towns filled with traditions and character.

Ted and I curiously explored these history-filled communities, stopping at weathered seafood shacks along the way for lobster rolls on toasted buns. We were enchanted by towns that seemed to spiral around white church steeples, stately town halls, and lopsided rotaries. Flags on street-corner memorials and flowers on ancient graveyards accessorized century-old buildings. Often, numbers such as 1821 or 1792 humbly stated not the street address on colonial homes but when the house had been built. My mind frolicked. What would it have been like to raise a family in the 1800s? What was life like for colonial women before our modern materialism? Was pilgrim and puritan simplicity a blessing? Or was it pure hardship? Were they content with what they had, or did they want for more? I mulled over these thoughts, thankful for the warmth of my seat heater and the GPS that directed us home.

Cushioning the town borders, Massachusetts has forty-eight thousand acres of salt marshes, dunes, coastal banks, wet meadows, bogs, and swamps. Ecosystems announce seasons with evening choirs of spring peepers and occasional clucks from passing wild turkeys. Damp habitats provide moist quarters for snapping, spotted, painted, and box turtles. For snakes and blue spotted salamanders. For the small, wild, highbush blueberries and bog-loving cranberries. Massachusetts ecosystems are also the perfect breeding grounds for free-love mosquitoes, carriers of Eastern Equine Encephalitis (EEE) and West Nile virus.

While EEE was first recognized in 1938, West Nile made headlines shortly after we moved to New England with our five-month-old Tanner. Not only did I have a baby, but I certainly hadn't grown up around these dangers, and I wanted to know what to look for. What if my precious boy was bitten by a defiled mosquito and I didn't know it? Would he stop breathing? Turn blue? According to the Center for Disease Control and Prevention, babies infected with West Nile virus would likely show no symptoms. Or, they could develop a fever, headaches, and fatigue. Or, one in 150 diagnosed would show stupor, disorientation, coma, tremors, convulsions, and paralysis. Fabulous. What mother wouldn't be horrified to hear about these symptoms? Who doesn't want to protect his or her child from stupor, tremors, and convulsions? Should I swaddle him in mosquito netting and force him to play inside for the rest of his childhood?

Through early summer, I thankfully managed to keep my fears from evolving into paranoia. Then, darn it, autumn news would fuel maternal worries again, as a child afflicted with West Nile virus was reported just one county over. A town paper would pay tribute to the passing of an elderly woman stricken with the disease. As dead birds were found in our own town, children were encouraged to spend their evening playtime inside. I realized my cautious attitude wasn't singular, as high schools delayed football games to protect players and fans alike. Town soccer programs cancelled the season outright due to mosquito activity at dusk. West Nile virus was close to home, but within a few short years, it quickly spread with swarms of cases detected across the United States. So much for pacifying my fears.

Fulfilling my duties as a protector, I vigorously infused bug repellant into the daily routine. This really wasn't too difficult since we were already adept at keeping Lyme disease at bay by warding off deer ticks. With all of its woodlands, New England has a large population of scampering, furry creatures, which bring with them ticks and thus Lyme disease. Knowing someone affected with West Nile virus is rare, but Lyme disease is more prevalent, and the connection feels closer. Every season stories increase. Tales of the cousin who recognized the bull's eye rash of Lyme disease. The co-worker with unexplained headaches and fatigue. The sister-in-law who sat on a park bench only to have a tick dig its head into the soft tissue on her hip. Now, stricken with memory loss, she deals with temporary paralysis of facial muscles.

Seasonally, I refreshed the supplies of bug repellant. I was drawn to summery plastic bottles containing DEET, the popular active chemical ingredient. The savvy marketing spoke to my hurried mind: *Grab me! I am kind, safe, and will protect your lil' chickadees and all their friends!* While unloading the car at home, I flipped the bottle over and glanced at the back. The bold, black font commanded:

- Harmful to humans and animals.
- Do not apply over cuts, wounds, or irritated skin.
- Do not apply to hands or near eyes and mouth of young children.
- Do not allow young children to apply this product.
- Use just enough repellent to cover exposed skin and/or clothing.
- Do not use under clothing.
- Avoid over-application of this product.
- After returning indoors, wash treated skin with soap and water.
- Wash treated clothing before wearing it again.
- Use of this product may cause skin reactions in rare cases.
- Do not spray in enclosed areas.
- To apply to face, spray on hands first and then rub on face.
- Do not spray directly onto face.[1]

Hey, and by the way, have a great mosquito-free time.

Okay. So maybe I didn't have to *read* the bottle, just *use* the bottle. Even my son instinctually understood to squint and hold his breath to avoid the mist cloud while standing in a scarecrow position. Our bodies—as well as the labels—pleaded for caution, but I was not listening.

What amazing lengths we go to in order to avoid those annoying pests! Not only do we spray tender, young limbs, we also fashionably accessorize our backyards. Cheesy, popsicle-shaped citronella candles decorate patio tables. Tiki torches adorn backyard perimeters, both flickering and repelling biting insects. Neighbors tuck propane-fueled, carbon dioxide emitting machines into far corners of the yard, luring mosquitoes' spiny legs and transparent wings onto sticky adhesive pads.

We can very often count on our local town government to help keep the buggers at bay. When a summer provided more than the average number of dead birds, we barely had time to close our windows before low-flying planes dropped Bacillus thuringiensis israelensis (Bti)

onto nearby wetlands. Bti is often referred to as the least toxic micro-bicide applied to wetlands to kill mosquito larvae before they develop. We can also request a drive-by skeeter-cide with pyrethroids. With a simple phone call, the county will cruise by at dawn and fog fine, synthetic mist into the air to control the nuisance. Like many insecticides, pyrethroids attack adult mosquitoes through nerve functions causing paralysis and eventually victorious death. Curious about these pyrethroids, I found these descriptions on the Environmental Protection Agency's website:

- Slight risk of acute toxicity to humans.
- Doesn't pose unreasonable risk to wildlife.
- Practically nontoxic to birds. Toxic to fish and bees.[2]

At first, the words "slight," and "practically" comforted me, affirming pyrethroids were perfectly safe; exactly what I wanted to hear. Then a deeper voice challenged, "*slight* risk" of "*acute toxicity*"? Isn't that a little like "kind of poisonous"? What exactly is an "unreasonable risk"? How do birds feel about "practically" next to "nontoxic"? Do pyrethroids simply leave those birds alive but with a slight limp or twisted beak? Is it only toxic if you touch it or breathe it? Or use it more than once? If it "doesn't pose an unreasonable risk to wildlife," there is still some kind of risk involved. Did the EPA construct a warning gentle enough to pacify manufacturers and yet consider this an ample warning to protect them from liability?*[3] It looked more and more as if I was on my own to keep my toddler safe. Along with the fish and bees.

When nostalgic "Remember When" emails compare past generations to modern helicopter parenting, I set to grumbling. The emails taunt

---

* From the EPA: "Although DEET's use has been implicated in seizures among children, the Agency believes that the incident data are insufficient to establish DEET as the cause of the reported effects. However, because of DEET's unusual use pattern (direct application to human skin and clothing) and its association with seizure incidents, the Agency believes it is prudent to require clear, common sense use directions and improved label warnings and restrictions on all DEET product labels."

Which left me, honestly, not very reassured.

how past generations didn't have to wear bike helmets, carry little bottles of magic soap, or reapply buckets of sunscreen every three hours. They played outside all day, unattended, and survived just fine. In today's world, being a Good Parent includes stocking an arsenal of spray-on-smear-on weapons. In addition to hand sanitizer and sunscreen, diaper bags now carry bug spray with DEET. Back-up supplies are conveniently stored in the garage with one bottle in the sports bag and two in the camper. Believe me, I too long to yell, "Come in for dinner when the street lights go on." Instead, when my husband and toddler headed out with an oversized plastic bat and baseball on a summer evening, I dutifully called out, "Bug spray!"

With no obvious alternatives, I continued with the outdoor ritual to the pulse of the seasons. Rainy springs transitioned into the humidity of summer, and I took all of these preventative steps to keep my family safe from West Nile and EEE. Stay away nasty, high-pitched disease carriers! My kids want to play summer evening tag! They want to play catch with Dad and perfect their tumbling cartwheels. I am the protector, hear me roar! My job was to shield bony ankles and kissable necks from the bloodsuckers. Smack! Slap! Scratch, scratch.

Yet, something about using the spray bugged me like an annoying grain of sand—small enough to be buried in routine but an agitation nonetheless. I despised the layering. Observing my friends spraying clouds of mist down the front and up the back of their babes reassured me not to push the status quo. I was just new to motherhood. Who was I to question the forms and functions of parenting? Looking back, many of my decisions were born out of mimicking peers, not by careful researching. It made sense. If I had four minutes to spare, I was going to spend them stealing a moment of slumber or wiping down counters, not surfing the Internet. The simple, protective gesture of applying bug repellant made me feel strangely uneasy, yet I did it because I was supposed to. It was a parental act performed out of love and care for my children, like tucking them into bed at night, providing them with healthy meals, and reminding them to look both ways before crossing the street. But with each application I sprayed on my little ones, that grain of sand set to itching me.

Eight years later and in my mommy time-out, I finally had time for listening to and trusting myself. I was no longer willing to let the grain of sand irritate me. Instead of chiming "It's just what we do," I challenged myself. I embarked on a retail safari, an urban hunt for bug spray alternatives. I went to my local mega-store determined to uncover options without having to drive forty minutes out of my way to the nearest holistic store. Lo and behold, right next to the traditional DEET products was an equally effective alternative made from gentle repellants like citronella, lemongrass, peppermint, and cedarwood. And, hallelujah, the price point was in the same range! I had discovered a safe, convenient, and affordable option for bug spray, without the harsh ingredients or a long drive with a Google map! I chucked three into my shopping cart and skipped down the aisle with delight.

My action of challenging DEET in my family's bug spray was not that of an alarmist, raising picket signs or shouting "Down with Poisons!" through a bullhorn. DEET was simply the instigator challenging me either to choose the status quo or to choose wiser.

I went on safari one day to ease a nagging in my heart about bug spray and stumbled into a vivid, parallel world of delicious options. That tiny, agitating grain of sand? Now a treasured pearl. If I could feel the thrill of empowerment by this one action, where else could I make little changes? What other products could I replace with healthier options? I didn't want to stop at just one, I hungered for more. It dawned on me that it was not the simple, protective gesture guarding against bites that was pestering my instincts. It wasn't even one product or one active ingredient. It was the convoluted layering of products with inherent slight risks, claiming "practically nontoxic" applied to our permeable body. It was the constant application. The complex layer after layer. "It's just what we do," was no longer an acceptable reason for me to use a product or perform an action—I would make decisions based on awareness and not manipulative marketing. I would choose wiser for my family and myself. I would select simpler to respect my body. I would find options.

And yes, there were options.

Thirsty To Learn

The trauma (and drama) of the four "big" chemo treatments were coming to a climactic end. I mustered a gracious smile and accepted accolades of, "*You did it! Can you believe it? This is the last one.*""*It's almost over! Hang in there!*" For friends and family, it had been a long five months. They were ready to move on. Despite my yearning for normalcy, I didn't want to move on. (It was a complex, ridiculous emotion I really didn't understand but was real nonetheless.) When Ted, the doctors, and I squeezed into the exam room for the final chemo game plan, it took only a few "congratulations" before I broke into pleading sobs. *Please don't take the chemos away. Keep giving them to me. The chemos, they keep IT away.* I gasped for air, and a box of tissues, standard in every oncology room, was passed over to me. *I will stay like this. If you take the meds away, the cancer will come back. Please just let me take the meds. I want to do my job. Raise my kids. I can do both—kids and chemo, I know I can.* Softly, reassuringly, and with a slight tone of, "Silly rabbit, Trix are for kids," they explained, "It's okay. The next two meds are just as impactful but with kinder side effects." Their voices elicited memories of encouraging my son Kyle to swim without the plastic arm floaties. *You can do this!* So, I started to paddle. Sniffling, I accepted the next line item of twelve weeks of concurrent medications—Taxol, woven with thirteen months of Herceptin.

While I wasn't ready to whoop it up, those around me deserved kudos. The following week, I hosted a glamorous "Chemi's" Award Ceremony in our family room. It was my goofy, Oscar-like award show to recognize those who took the brunt of my journey: my family. With ridiculous insistence, I dressed in my 1986 teal Homecoming gown and knit hat, and my kids lined the couch in Sears clip-on ties and Disney princess costume couture. Neither paparazzi nor my digital Cannon Rebel was allowed, as I presented three plastic trophies to my children. For each, I celebrated seemingly tiny gestures that were invaluable to me. How they came home off the bus and ran upstairs just to ask how I was doing. How they took care of each other, occasionally making lunches as a team on days I stayed in bed upstairs. How they looked me right in my dark, circled eyes, and with unconditional love and sincerity told me I was beautiful.* The small wins that often blend into the background are worthy of celebration. Appreciating the tiniest gestures they had done for me, I awarded each child a trophy and a bear hug, while siblings applauded.

Later, as my children went out to ride bikes, leaving dress-up clothes strewn across the hallway, Ted gave me a gift, revealing something he had kept to himself since my diagnosis. As we sat on the couch, he quietly shared that my diagnosis evoked a fear in him deeper than he ever expected or even knew existed. His instinctual reaction was to become the rock in the family, maintaining constancy and stability in the midst of our collective emotions and anxiety. While I had focused solely on surviving, he had focused on keeping the family together. During that afternoon celebration, my binder paper was not invited. I left it upstairs while I savored this day with my family. With this small ritual of love, my family had my blessing to move forward.

With the start of the "kinder" meds of Taxol and Herceptin, the number of doctors' appointments eased. I was eager to focus on simmering questions about products I used. I decided to begin by reading product labels. For what? I didn't quite know. I was pretty sure the words "slightly poisonous" and "kinda harmful" wouldn't be listed on the labels, but wouldn't my intuition kick in? Maybe I would come across an ingredient and get a sixth sense, a foreboding feeling in my gut that would

* When volunteering in school classrooms, it was striking how children would take one look at the cancer garb and move right on, asking me to tie shoes or zip their jackets. Children are so beautifully non-judgmental. They simply saw Mrs. Marsh. That, or maybe I'd always looked haggard?

tell me to choose another product. Maybe the bottle would pulse in my hand, or I'd hear an audible voice in my head saying, "No, not that one."

Determined, I set out for the beauty care aisles of my local Target. I picked up the first product, glanced at the packaging, and waited for my Spidey sense to tingle and inform me whether this was the right product. After a few seconds, I realized I would have to do it the hard way. My mind ran its tongue curiously over label fonts trying to comprehend the meanings of *toxin free*, *natural*, *eco-health*, *chemical free*, and *organic*. I rotated bottles to view the contents listed in tiny print. I had never asked my peers what they thought about ingredients because I was too insecure pronouncing the foreign terms. Embarrassingly, I had assumed the product lists on the back were scientific words for ingredients found in the natural world, like sodium chloride (table salt). It turns out many of these difficult-to-pronounce words were chemicals that didn't translate into any type of natural product I knew about.

Utmost faith escorted me by the elbow whenever I shopped. A pretty font with swirly, green vines wrapped around the word *natural* on the front side of a lotion was my reassurance I could safely slather it on my little one's dry, winter skin. A company would never knowingly use harmful ingredients, would it? Isn't it illegal or prohibited somehow? I was naive to say the least, but I didn't want to let that stop me from my mission. Still, how does someone with only a high school sophomore chemistry background begin to decipher ingredients? It did not sound interesting. At all. It was looking more and more like a lot of work and a huge time-suck.

In a moment of serendipity, I found a tiny ad in our town paper. The Children's Museum down the road was hosting a workshop for families on nontoxic living. My heart committed instantly to attending, but my brain was skeptical. My busy life resisted change. Voices inside my head argued, *Why is no one else changing?* I felt like a proactive parent—affixing child safety latches on cabinet doors and setting up gates at the top of stairs. Wouldn't I know about household toxins if such things existed?

I pacified my internal struggle by inviting two girlfriends to attend with me. We would decide for ourselves by turning it into an evening out.

The presenters, two authors who had written a book on nontoxic living, hoped to provide awareness on harmful ingredients in household products. Sadly, it wasn't the simple, informative, use-this-not-that message I had hoped to hear. Frustration and fear descended on the small, wide-eyed audience who interpreted their warnings as doom and gloom. They didn't have picket signs advertising, "The end is near," but they may as well have. Apparently, my ignorant parenting decisions were causing the world to slowly cave into itself and mutant children to be born with six fingers and toes. Very soon, society would consist of a mass of genetically modified, toxic waste creatures.

Okay, perhaps it wasn't quite that doomy, but it was gloomy, and honestly, more than my mind could handle. The last thing I needed was more parental fear. On the back of a bank receipt I found in the bottom of my purse, I tried scribbling many of the harmful ingredients mentioned during the meeting. BPA, parabens, BHT (I put a question mark next to it-what did it stand for?), chlorine bleach (was this the same bleach I used on my laundry?), pthal–something. Scribbling around the corner and onto the front, I wrote a reminder to check nail polishes for three unnecessary ingredients: toluene, formaldehyde, and DBP (what on earth?). By the end of the evening, I was confused and overwhelmed.

Later in the week while grocery shopping, I pulled out the crumpled list to make a good-faith effort toward this new way of life. Standing in the shampoo aisle, I adjusted my eyes to the tiny print on the back of bottles. My list said I should avoid *coal tar*, a known human carcinogen. Okay. It was prominently listed in the shampoo I was holding. I put it back and reached for another. This brand had it too. Sigh. Okay. Skip to another harmful ingredient then: *parabens*. No parabens in this product! Wait, yes, *methylparaben*. Was this the same? I didn't understand. I felt defeated. Deep breaths—think. The children's shampoo advertised the word "natural" on the front but had almost every word from my no-no list. I'm not typically a person who swears, but this task had me muttering, *What the hell?*

My feet started to feel like blocks of concrete; the gears in my brain were stuck. Kaytee was now sitting in the cart, squishing the bread with cans of soup out of boredom. I wanted to snap at her, but she was not the cause of my frustration. How was I supposed to start changing when it was this difficult to find one "safe" product on the shelf? How much time do these people think I have? Years of shopping experience and mother-hood-frustration took over. I grabbed the most economical brand under the yellow sale sign and chucked it into the cart. With remorse and guilt, I pushed the cart to the checkout line. I pouted over missing the thrill of empowerment. I felt inundated with too much information, yet at the same time, not enough.

For two weeks, I stewed over my indecision, allowing each lathering of the shampoo to remind me of my non-action. The impatient part of me wanted to ignore what I had learned. I could continue to shop according to coupons, sales, and name brands; at least I was being fiscally responsible. As Director of Household Consumerism, I took pride in my proficient shopping skills and was deeply comfortable knowing which aisle and which shelves my favorite brands resided. I could stop feeling as though I was challenging the advent of the wheel and just get on with the process of living. Ignorance could be my way out, and my shopping-induced anxiety would be eliminated.

But that's not what I promised myself. It's not what I promised to do for my family. As frustrating as it felt, I had cancer, and having cancer gave me time. If I could find the resolve to fight the big "C," surely I could find the fortitude to learn a new trick. Decipher some words. Figure it out. What was this, really, compared to chemo?

As providence would have it, I came across an evening program called *Chronicle*. This particular episode featured established local authors, Philip and Alice Shabecoff and their book, *Poisoned Profits: The Toxic Assault on Our Children*. With educated passion, the Shabecoffs presented a dismal, yet mesmerizing look at environmental toxins. *Chronicle* then balanced the story with input from regional experts, including a pediatrician and green scientists. The representative defending synthetic chemicals seemed to have a condescending message, which offended me. Wait, no. Royally pissed me off. What I heard the chemical rep say, was that mothers needed to focus on helmets and car seats, not on harmful chemicals. It wasn't our job. Her patronizing remarks lit me on fire. I *was* focused on helmets! I *was* focused on car seats! Was she deriding my parenting? My ability to protect my most precious possessions? Did she underestimate my maternal passion? Once again, primitive emotion rose from deep within me, a source of strength that propelled me past my insecurities. I was ready. Bring. It. On.

Poor pro-chemical rep on *Chronicle*. She will never know the spark she ignited with her belittling tone and her offhand remark. It breathed flames into a revolution. A turning point in my journey. She'll never know what she started. But I thank her.

Pumped with spiritual adrenalin, my core chanted, *Knowledge is responsibility...knowledge is responsibility*. My inner voice knew there was substance to the community workshop's message, and my curiosity took charge. My mind snapped alive with questions. Haven't we been using household cleaners and cosmetics and eating food forever? What makes now different from any other century? Why is this growing movement I have stumbled into encouraging me to change my ways? When it came down to it, I wanted to know *why* toxins entered my home, my body, and my children's bodies, without my having a say in the matter.

The Missing Piece

Voracious to understand, yet without a chemist in the family tree to call, I turned to reading. The search for information took time, and for that matter, it wasn't always easy or positive. Academic articles and science reports became unlikely companions with my morning tea. Websites for nonprofit organizations, such as Women's Voices for the Earth (WVE) and Environmental Working Group (EWG), provided stepping-stones from one insight to another. While searching the Internet, I was comforted to find other women blogging about quests similar to mine. I made constant trips to the library and anxiously awaited the neat, rectangular boxes of books I ordered online as I sought to fill my brain with information. Some books preached through doom-colored glasses, and I immediately set them aside. Other books ripped my mind open and filled it with brilliant illumination. After only a few months, cockeyed piles of well-loved books with warped covers, dog-eared pages, and cryptic, penciled notes begging to be re-read surrounded me.

As a domestic archeologist, I slowly uncovered the information I craved. The puzzle pieces were shifting into place in my mind; the picture was beginning to come together. My "a-ha" moments built the frame, moments of clarity cemented the corners, and my constant reading filled in the image. I kept picking up one particular piece repeatedly, fingering it, and tapping it on the table. How did it fit in? It was a number recurring in my research, one with little significance to me. It was the number 83,000, referencing the number of inventoried synthetic chemicals. Was I supposed to be scared? The number was so unfathomable; my mind kept trying to file it under Unnecessary Information. Yet, the number kept reappearing, haunting me, triggering a sinister villain soundtrack when I came across it in my reading. Obviously, it begged for my attention.

I scanned the chemical science timeline for a place to immerse myself. I could start as far back as Ancient Egypt, when they mixed together compounds for cosmetics. Or I could jump in after the Plague bombarded medieval Europe, resulting in advances in medicine. It was the late 1800s, though, which created a convenient entry point to learning, when European chemists started synthesizing molecules that did not exist in nature. As we turned the corner of the century, World War I and World War II increased the demand for chemical resources.*

....
* The process of distilling petroleum, produced descendants of tar, benzene, naphthalene, and gasoline. Vinyl chloride gas, born a century ago, evolved into the polyvinyl chloride (PVC) of today, sporting its own identifiable #3 recycle code on plastics, clothing, and building materials. Acetone, neoprene, polyethylene, nylon, and toluene are some of the substances that were invented or discovered around these decades. I never paid attention to them before but found I regularly used them in our home.

As peacetime descended, petrochemicals and plastics revamped domestic life with new products. Poisonous gases were repurposed into insecticides, pesticides, and fertilizers. The daunting name polytetrafluoroethylene (PTFE) became popular under Teflon. Polystyrene found uses in radios, clocks, packaging, insulation, and electrical equipment. Celluloid and Bakelite, the first synthetic plastics, became part of clothing, kitchenware, and ping-pong balls. Super glues, Formica, and Saran Wrap became household jargon. Tide, with its clean new scent, changed laundry forever as the first heavy-duty detergent based on synthetic compounds. Through these products and many others like them, the synthetic chemical movement had successfully infiltrated our homes and our culture.*

What I consider quality of life—convenience, price point, and choice—is largely a result of the synthetic chemical revolution. An emergency pair of nylons on the way to work? Convenience store. Children's pain medicine at two a.m.? I can name eight pharmacies within five minutes. Shopping for two weeks' worth of boxed and frozen foods?† Heck, I don't even have to leave my house; I can have it delivered right after Grey's Anatomy. What an opulent, lavish world I live in! Everything is at my fingertips. Our choices are so diverse; entire aisles are devoted to products that didn't even exist for the colonial women who once occupied this town. Soda. Breakfast cereals. Bleached paper goods. Red, blue, and green sports drinks. Plug-in air fresheners heavily scented with cinnamon apples and vanilla fields.

This is my life. We want what we want when we want it. We want it year round and in every town. And we can have it. I had never thought to stop and question, *is* our excessiveness the right choice? Why would I? This was the world I was born into. It's all I've known.

....
* The proliferation of synthetic chemicals grew rapidly in the late 1800s, resulting in the founding of the American Chemical Society in 1876. In 1888, Massachusetts Institute of Technology recognized the movement and created the first Chemical Engineering curriculum.

† Synthetic preservatives, found in many boxed and frozen foods, extend product shelf life, allowing us to ship farther and store longer. I can find butylated hydroxytoluene (BHT) listed on the box of cereal at breakfast, on the frozen pizza for lunch, and again on my tube of lipstick, in each instance preserving the fats and oils within.

Thankfully, someone wiser was deeply concerned, could not bear to be silent, and passionately spoke up. In 1962, Rachel Carson, an ecologist-biologist-author, published the book, *Silent Spring*. It was the first book to raise awareness of the interaction between chemical usage and its effect on our environment. Rachel Carson was deeply disturbed by the irresponsible manner in which we used chemicals without understanding the long-term effects. Through *Silent Spring*, she challenged our society and government to question our prolific chemical use. Carson described how, in such a fraction of time, humans have altered the dynamics of their surroundings:

> To a large extent, the physical form and the habits of the earth's vegetation and its animal life have been molded by the environment. Considering the whole span of earthly time, the opposite effect, in which life actually modifies its surroundings, has been relatively slight. Only within the moment of time represented by the present century has one species—man—acquired significant power to alter the nature of his world.[4]

My father, a geology hobbyist, demonstrated by extending his arm-span from his six-foot frame, stating, "This is Earth's timeline, fingertip to fingertip." Turning his head toward his right hand, he continued, "If you take an emery board and swipe my fingernail once (with his forefinger wiggling), that one swipe would erase the human timeline." To Rachel's point, within dust particles of that swipe lies just one century, during which we allowed powerful synthetic chemicals to recklessly alter animal species, plant life, and entire intricate ecosystems.

How I wish I could have invited Rachel Carson to dinner! Sat down with her over an arugula salad and conversed about the plight of robins, elm trees, and sagebrush shared in *Silent Spring*. What would it have been like to have insight on the relationship between nature and our bodies at a time when the terms *pollution*, *green*, or *eco*-anything, were barely concepts?

Maybe we would have ended our meal with a cup of tea and moved to the fireplace. I would have asked what it was like to speak out as a writer—to say nothing about being a woman—against monolithic industries in the 1950s and 60s. What did it feel like to swim upstream against science that proudly advanced American pop culture? No doubt, I would have sat in stunned silence as she shared how chemical manufacturers ran ads telling Americans to ignore *Silent Spring*. And how she wisely responded to them, "As you listen to the present controversy about pesticides, I recommend that you ask yourself: Who speaks? And why?"[5]

This invitation to supper will never happen, as Rachel Carson lost her battle with breast cancer in 1964 at age fifty-seven. In the decade following her death, the United States continued to produce synthetic chemicals. During the 1970s, an average of six hundred new compounds were introduced to the market *every* year.

Fortunately, those who had been listening eventually took action. Congress passed the Clean Air Act, the first successful attempt at creating national standards to control air pollution,[6] and the Clean Water Act, which established new regulations for water.[7] In 1976, while I was playing with hula-hoops and big wheels in the cul-de-sac until bedtime with no bug spray on, President Ford signed into law the Toxic Substance Control Act, or TSCA (referred to as "tocsa"). It was a radical document publicly acknowledging links between environmental hazards and health, which also created an inventory of chemicals. I clicked on a press release from the then-EPA Administrator expounding on our government's shift in thinking:

> ...we know so little—so abysmally little—about these chemicals. We know little about their health effects, especially over the long term at low levels of exposure. We know little about how many humans are exposed, and how and to what degree. We do not even know precisely how many—much less precisely

which—new chemical compounds are made and marketed every year.

It brought tears to my eyes to realize this proclamation was almost forty years old. We really *did* know better, didn't we? Then another sentence caught my eye:

> .. the Toxic Substances Control Act is "one of the most important pieces of 'preventive medicine' legislation" ever passed by Congress. The legislation represents a major step toward an increasingly effective preventive approach toward the 'environmental disease' that has been called the 'disease of the century.'[8]

Oh, thank you, leaders of my childhood! So much was cocooned in TSCA's intentions! On the year of our bicentennial, we were taking a stand, enacting profound legislation, protecting our people, our bodies, and our beautiful American environment. I love our country—our progressive leaders willing to stand up for its children. Like a season finale, I wanted to know what happened next. What did we do? Tell me, what did we accomplish? I know I was alive then, but Sesame Street was my main source of current events, updating me on the antics of the letter Q. I had to re-live this as an adult.

I followed the trail rather quickly. In 1978, polychlorinated biphenyls (PCBs) were banned under TSCA.* The United States finally had a system in place to ban them. [9] Applause!

The use of synthetic chemicals in our products existed, albeit silently, way before I was born. This movement shifted us from the multi-functional ingredients our great-grandparents used to the foreign-to-pronounce ingredients and a disposable product-for-every-use that we have today. While we *have* been cleaning homes, using cosmetics, eating and drinking throughout human history, it is only in the last

....
* PCBs have been shown to cause skin cancer, reproductive failures, gastric disorders, skin lesions, and other serious effects in laboratory animals. Reportedly odorless and tasteless, I wonder who volunteered to taste test it.

six decades that have we been inundating our bodies daily with thousands of substances never encountered before the twentieth century.

I only had a narrow, self-centered understanding of what existed since 1970, or even really, since the mid-1980s, when I became a teenage card-carrying consumer, purchasing McDonald's lunches and Obsession perfume on my own. I have a hard time understanding how Ma on *Little House on the Prairie*, one of my favorite childhood shows, kept her one-room house so spiffy without blue window spray and disinfecting, lemon-scented floor cleaner. Did the upstanding citizens of Walnut Grove deal with asthma, allergies, autism, or attention disorders with common familiarity? Were any of those words even in their vocabulary? How in the world did their farm animals grow large enough to eat without hormones and antibiotics? How did Pa nurture successful crops without synthetic fertilizers and pesticides? Why are those ingredients so widely used today?

My self-questioning made me feel reluctant. If I swayed from what I was raised on, would I put my family in danger? Without the list of chemicals on the back of my counter spray, would it be effective? Would I encourage swine-flu-inducing countertops? Would straying from mainstream choices lead to eating salmonella-tainted suppers with decaying teeth? The lost feeling in the pit of my stomach was like a young love break-up. I had trusted so unconditionally, so fully. I had never thought to question. I could feel imminent change, but writhing and wiggling out of my comfortable skin toward understanding would take time.

Understanding the momentum of the synthetic chemical revolution was essential for me. Trying to regurgitate it was twice the struggle. I had to reduce the information to Kristi-checklist style and big-picture events:

❖ Post World War eras saw the advancement of synthetic chemicals and integrated them into our society. Their benefits catapulted easier living through variety and affordability.

❖ Rachel Carson energized environmentalism by challenging our prolific use of these substances without understanding the complete ramifications to our bodies and our environment.

❖ Her shadow reached out and infused 1970s culture. With the EPA established, PCBs were banned under TSCA. (Enough letters... now *I'm* starting to sound like Sesame Street.)

Then, there it was. I spotted the number again, only this time its ominous weight made sense. The mystery behind the 83,000 reference unfolded. The chemical inventory system swelled over my lifetime to the unfathomable inventory of nearly 83,000 chemicals. I found myself holding my breath as I absorbed a just-as-staggering number: 62,000 synthetic chemicals were simply grandfathered in when TSCA was created. Complete toxicological screening data are available for just seven percent of these chemicals, leaving more than ninety percent that have never been tested for their effects on human health.[10]

TSCA failed to protect public health to its potential. In my teen years, TSCA's assertiveness weakened, and since its inception, has only banned a whopping five chemicals. Instead of requiring that all chemicals be proven safe before usage, the United States produces or imports forty-two billion pounds of chemicals annually.[11] Annually. Instead of reducing the inventory of toxic chemicals, we pump, circulate, absorb, and burn unknowns into our world. While TSCA seemed to be the panacea at first, disillusionment hit me, as I realized it wasn't really protecting us.

Deep, slow exhale.

Fortunately, other governments are blazing protective trails in varying degrees, insisting on bans and regulations. Through *Exposed*, a book by Mark Schapiro, I learned how our lax leadership on environmental regulation leaves a choice, "either to adapt to Europe's more aggressive standards for protecting the health of its citizens, or risk losing what is now the biggest and most affluent market in the world."[12] Schapiro states:

The frequent result is that the European Union and the United States review the same scientific studies, have access to the same toxicity data and come to entirely different conclusions. The European approach is called the precautionary principle, and the result is that many substances now banned in Europe are in wide use in the United States.[13]

In the personal care products industry alone, the European Union has banned eleven hundred ingredients.[14] The United States has banned only nine.[15] It is business as usual; companies that sell to both sides of the ocean adapt to separate regulations. It's a little bit like opening the passenger door and buckling your son in with a kiss on the cheek, while letting his brother play freely in the back seat. Why isn't the same rule applied to both? Many companies are making two batches—one with safer ingredients and one without them.

But enough. I am constantly telling my children whining won't get them anywhere. The bittersweet news I can take from Schapiro's message is that if we were to commit to using safer ingredients today, it wouldn't take decades to develop new formulas and secret-pressed-powder recipes. Last I heard, people strolling the Champs-Élysées in Paris didn't have mangy, greasy hair or smell like a cattle farm on a warm day. When governmental regulations state that carcinogenic and mutagenic ingredients are prohibited, the Europeans still find ways to use deodorant, shampoo, and hand soaps. Their women still wear makeup. It's Europe, for heaven's sake—the epicentre of all things stylish and couture. Do you think those women are going to give up their lipstick? Puh-leaze.

Many options already exist. We just need the correct legislation to outlaw those same eleven hundred chemicals in our products as well. Here in the United States, we *should also* have the freedom to live without fear of the unknown.

Lab Rats

One particular evening, my learning curve was electrified by an unexpected moment. As a young breast cancer patient, I was invited to

33

share my experience with college girls. As I drove to Bridgewater State University, I was cranky. It had been a busy day with a rushed evening. The pile of dirty dishes left abandoned as I raced out the door weighed in my mind. I grumbled, *Why did I volunteer to do this? What am I, a zoo animal on display? I'm not any fricken' different from them.* But I knew better. I used to be them. I used to think cancer was for Others. I sharply reprimanded myself. *Maybe this event is not about you. Maybe there is a reason you are supposed to be there. Pull up your big girl panties, stand tall, be kind, be genuine, and learn something.*

The audience *was* curious about what I had endured, but instead of gawking as I feared, they were empathetic. Silently, I made note of my surging adrenalin. I was relishing the opportunity to guide women along my journey, watching their glistening eyes light with awareness. In my mind, a thought flickered: *maybe I didn't ask for cancer, but what if I could help others?* I tucked the notion away for another day, wrapped up my presentation, and moved to the audience to listen to the remaining speakers. Within ten minutes, I realized the reason I was there was bigger than sharing my story. The shocking information I listened to connected me to my next life level.

Laura Sparks, representing the Massachusetts Breast Cancer Coalition (MBCC), shared breath-taking data. The presentation illustrated the risk of being diagnosed with breast cancer in third-world countries, compared to industrialized countries, and what happened to those numbers as women immigrated to our country.

- The highest rates of breast cancer are found in the industrialized nations of North America and Western Europe, while lower rates are generally found in western Asia, southern Africa, and South America.[16]
- Women who move from countries with low breast cancer rates to industrialized countries soon acquire the higher risk of their new country.[17]
- In many countries that are industrializing or in transition, breast cancer rates are escalating sharply.[18]

For example, women from Asian countries, where the rates are four to seven times lower than the United States, who immigrate to our country, experience an eighty percent increase in risk after living here a decade or more. A generation later, the risk for their daughters approaches that of American-born women.[19]

Stunned was an understatement. My eyes darted back and forth across her PowerPoint presentation. You mean the statistic of one in eight women diagnosed with breast cancer didn't apply to women across the planet? What would cause variances? What was the correlation between industrialized countries and the staggering data? Apparently, women must pay a price when deciding to move to the United States seeking an opportunity to chase the American Dream. Are any women even familiar with this statistic? Rogue genes you could blame. Risk factors like lack of exercise and poor nutrition felt generic. These new studies created a different picture. I felt a bubbling, sickening panic, *Why aren't these statistics common knowledge?* I was infuriated—desperate to somehow share them with my friends.

After the presentation, I thanked the hosts for inviting me to participate, honored for the chance to share my story. I then sought out Laura. I babbled about how I was in awe of her presentation and the data she shared. I suggested the MBCC presentation could be shared home-party style, reaching out to women where they could learn in the comfort of their own living rooms surrounded by friends. For the first time, I experienced an urgency to educate. I wanted to share, talk, and yell out. But how? I'm no scientist. I'm not a professor. I'm not affiliated with the MBCC and hadn't researched any data. I didn't even own a pair of un-scuffed pumps to wear. Once again, I had so much information swarming inside my head that by the time I arrived home, I was unable to regurgitate what I had learned to my husband. And that's saying something.

After that evening, I became convinced that some cancer statistics are so ubiquitous, they should be memorized along with the Pledge of Allegiance and our National Anthem:

❖ In just two generations, from 1950-2001, the rate of all child-hood cancers of all types leapt sixty-seven percent.[20]

❖ Between 1973 and 1998, breast cancer incidence rates in the United States increased by more than 40 percent.[21]

❖ In the United States, men have slightly less than a one in two lifetime risk for cancer.[22]

❖ For women, the risk is a little more than one in three.[23]

❖ In the United States, cancer accounts for one in four deaths.[24]

So this is life, eh? We learn to crawl and ride a bike. Enter puberty, go to college, get married; maybe strive for balance as a young mother. Celebrate our forties and hug a girlfriend as she faces a discovered tumor. Grieve for a family member who passes away from a rare diagnosis. Prepare for retirement with complacency, knowing many of us will be diagnosed with one of over two hundred types of cancers.* Is this Generation X's destiny? †

To be fair, it wasn't just cancer statistics exploding in my generation. There were also unprecedented rates of other illnesses and disabilities:

❖ More than one third of American children now have autism, allergies, ADHD, or asthma.[25]

❖ Asthma is increasing every year in the United States. The number of people diagnosed with asthma grew by 4.3 million from 2001 to 2009.[26]

❖ Food allergies among children in the United States are becoming more common over time. This has resulted in a 265% increase in the rate of hospitalizations related to food allergic reactions.[27]

....

* According to the American Cancer Society's Cancer Facts and Figures, "most cancers do not result from inherited genes but from damage (mutation) to genes that occur during one's lifetime. Mutations may result from internal factors such as hormones or the metabolism or nutrients within cells, or external factors such as tobacco, chemicals and sunlight."

† Maybe not for the Millennium generation, as their outline is being re-drafted with obesity rates thrown in. For the first time in history, they face the probability of having a shorter life span than their parents.

❖ Nearly one-third of United States children were at risk or obese at nine months of age and at two-years-old.[28] (Before they started playing video games and celebrating good grades with a drive-through window meal.)

Like a horror movie I hate but cannot stop watching, I found this information both revolting and compelling. Some moments my eyes were wide open, I could hardly breathe, and I couldn't put the information down. Other times my heart sank, and my throat tightened as I read the data confirming that childhood cancers once considered a rarity is no longer the case.

Whether Generation X, Y, or Z, our society should not bear the burden of becoming a statistic *before* environmental exposures are determined harmful. Companies, manufacturers, and our government, should *first* have to prove a chemical or ingredient has long-term safety before it is used. Right now, we are a laboratory in the making. You, me, us—we provide the statistics. Our lifestyles will be analyzed, crunched, and keyed into future PowerPoints. This data, the x and y, have the answers. My focus was becoming more intense: I wanted to choose which group of statistics I fell into; the category labeled non-smoking, sunscreen-applying, reduced-exposure-to-harmful-chemicals group. Stick that on my family tree.

I'd had enough of my heavy history lesson for now. I forced myself to unplug my computer, walk onto my deck, and face the sun. I needed to shift the heaviness in order to focus.*

Take Me Home

Inundated with statistics, I shifted into speed-reading mode and skimmed through *Silent Spring's* section on insecticides. My eyes ran

---

* This chapter is heavy on the data and gloom. Feel free to go for a walk as well, but please do come back. Once through this section—as important as it is—the story gets livelier. Promise.

over words I could pronounce but not comprehend. Phrases such as "substituting one atom of chlorine for one of hydrogen" blended, putting me into high school chemistry clock-watching stupor. Then, in chapter four, Rachel Carson snapped me back to attention with one declaration: "The answer is to be found in the amazing history of Clear Lake, California."

Clear Lake, California? Was she talking about *my* Clear Lake? The scene of so many childhood memories for me and my family? Why, Clear Lake and I go *way* back!

In the early 1980s, my parents, my brother, and I camped through the jewels of the Pacific Coast, including Big Sur, Bodega Bay, and Clear Lake. Our station wagon towed a pop-up tent trailer, while John Denver crooned of country roads and sunshine on shoulders from eight-track tapes. My memories of Clear Lake—rumored to be the oldest lake in North America—involved the scent of morning bacon arousing me from sleeping bag warmth, spaghetti dinners, and roasting marsh-mallows while singing John Jacob Jingleheimer Schmidt. I still have the faded photo of my ten-year-old self, wearing orange short-shorts with a Snoopy emblem, standing thigh-high in wheat-colored grass, my puffy blonde hair and freckled face squinting into the summer sun. During our stay, I hiked, collected rocks and participated in the State Park Junior Ranger program. Female park rangers, sporting Smokey Bear ranger hats, became my summer role models. They led afternoon classes on how to decipher animal scat or how to identify sleek, red-twisted Manzanita branches. I certainly wasn't thinking about what might be in the water I accidentally swallowed while swimming or the infamous gnaticide history of Clear Lake. Rachel Carson now explained in chapter four what had been unknown to our family back in the days of my Snoopy shorts.

In 1949, the almost invisible gnat—Chaoborus astictopus—had congregated thickly, annoying year-round residents and driving away tourists. These zipping little bothers did not carry diseases or suck your blood. They more likely interrupted enthralling, campfire ghost stories by flying into the mouths of storytellers and buzzing in the ears of listeners. Swatting away these tiny specks was such a dreadful annoyance, the people of the time elected to annihilate the gnats with dichlorodiphenyldichloroethane (DDD). Reading Carson's description, I became wary. Not because DDD had more letters than our alphabet, but due to DDD's pedigree as a probable carcinogen. At the time, the DDD was diluted to one part per seventy million parts water.* After the first application, testing revealed no DDD could be found in the lake. By the second application, the near-decimation of the gnats was thought to be successful. Ghost stories resumed. Residents enjoyed the outdoors without the pesky hand waving in front of their faces. I envisioned the workers who applied the DDD brushing dirt off their hands, self-praising, "Yep that'll do it."

Is your mind foreshadowing what happened next? Do you assume DDD left a catastrophic trail, re-gifting harm from tiny plants, to tiny bugs, to tiny fish? Hijacking its way through fatty tissues of the food chain? If so, you are a quick study and would have assumed correctly. I speculated the same and skimmed to the end of chapter four. I wasn't being cynical; in fact, I really am more of a rose-colored-glasses girl. Maybe I am desensitized from the endless news headlines of my world. The relationship between chemicals, humans, and environment leaves numerous wildlife tragedies: chemically castrated frogs, two headed fish, Beluga whales with stomach and liver cancer, and thinning eggshells of Brown Pelicans and Peregrine Falcons. Stories which leave me feeling helpless are so common in our news; it is easy to grow slightly numb.

Resuming *Silent Spring's* tale a half century ago, Carson explained that the DDD used to kill gnats had not disappeared. It "merely had gone into the fabric of the life the lake supports." [29] One notable casualty was the black and white Western Grebe, a bird with a slender, curving neck, found to be "loaded with DDD in extraordinary concentration of sixteen-hundred parts per million." Now I am not sure what that looks like, but we do know that eleven years after the first application

....
* What does one part per seventy million look like? If you were to line up seventy million three-inch wide wine glasses, fill just one of those wine glasses with Pinot Noir and the rest with water, they would stretch for 3,314 miles, roughly the equivalent of my move from Seattle to Boston.

of DDD at Clear Lake, more than one thousand pairs of Western Grebe had diminished to approximately thirty.

Putting the book down, I closed my eyes. Clear Lake's lesson was not shocking to me. It was consistent with the life I had come to know. Something else pulsed underneath Carson's message. Was it the human need to decimate annoyances in favor of convenience that pulled at me? No. Control over gnats—or grubs, ants, dandelions, clover, termites, crabgrass—that's just what we do, season after season. And if we don't, our neighbors do. What was compelling to me was the societal "a-ha" moment Carson created by combining her biologist background with eloquent writing. She taught us that matter doesn't just disappear, but accumulates from one species to another over time. The fate of the Western Grebe illustrates bioaccumulation to the reading masses. Bioaccumulation—the accumulation of substances, in this case, up the food chain—is well accepted now but was a paradigm shift just fifty itsy-bitsy years ago. Why do I get so excited reading about these things?

Because we *learn*, and this is consoling. Knowledge empowered us in the 1970s when our country took actions to reduce lead levels, phase out leaded gasoline, and ban it in household paint. As a result, lead levels in the blood of American children have dropped by eighty-six percent since the late 1970s.[30] In the 1980s, awareness among my parents' demographics rippled, changing their hair-spraying ways and discouraging the use of aerosol cans containing chlorofluorocarbons (CFCs). Shortly after the United Nation's unparalleled cooperation, somewhere above our planet, the thinning of the ozone layer appears to have started to rebound.[31] Environmental health grassroots movements have spread like wildfire since *Silent Spring*. Now, every morning I can scan dozens of updates to learn what the United States and other countries are doing to combat or encourage environmental issues. We have more information now than ever before, and progress is hope. Holding my copy of *Silent Spring*, I shouted silently and danced inwardly. We do learn.

NEW DAWN

I have continued the camping tradition of my youth with my own children, hoping to provide fond memories for them in the future, while still allowing myself to re-live bits of my own childhood. One camping escapade brought me face-to-face with rather persistent bio-accumulative villains—PCBs. The same chemicals I had previously high-fived over for being banned. This particular camping trip was a step for my children toward becoming independent fishing people; meaning, I don't fish. My children can untangle fishing line and hook bait 'till their little hearts are content, but it is not my camping thing. I am happy to observe, monitor, and support them while leafing through a magazine article, enjoying the afternoon breeze. Rangers of this Connecticut campground instructed us not to eat any fish from the lake, attributing the danger to pesticides used by nearby farmers. Because of the pesticide warning, I kept a watchful eye on the kids and instructed them only to fish and kayak, but not to swim. Because of my buzz-kill-no-swim-policy, I did end up kicking off my flip-flops and diving in fully clothed to rescue half of my daughter's fishing pole when it broke off and flung like a dart into four-foot-deep water. "Stay there! I'll get it!" I yelled, taking one for my young team. I grabbed the pole off the slimy, muddy lake bottom in an effort to maintain the camping peace and avoid emotional devastation. We all know what happens when two siblings have what a third does not; it's a riot in the making. While I would have preferred not to be swimming in potentially pesticide-contaminated waters, I sure as heck wasn't going to let them go in after the broken pole, as we still had three days left of camping. I'm a mom. I do what I have to do.

After the fact, I discovered in a pamphlet at a local fishing supply store, that this waterway, along with many others, was being watched not for farm runoff, but for levels of skin penetrating PCBs. Evidently many chemicals, even if banned three decades before, are persistent and highly stable. This means they break down extremely slowly over time and can lurk in our soils, waterways, and buildings. PCBs fall into a category of chemicals referred to as PBT: persistent, bioaccumulative, and toxic. Since fish absorb PCBs in their fatty tissues, the literature

41

recommended limiting the amount of fish to eat. It also suggested trimming away the fat and cooking it on a rack so that any remaining fat would drip away. Unfortunately for my children, their fishing energy failed to produce any dinner for us; although if it had, I wouldn't have let them eat it. We were a catch-and-release fishing family. While I appreciated the cooking tips from the flyer, the larger lesson was a waving red flag: we must still alter our behavior—taking precautions to protect ourselves from a chemical banned thirty years prior. [32]

Today, biomonitoring is a tool scientists can use to determine the amount (and types) of chemicals and toxins present in humans and wildlife. Analyzing samples of urine, blood, saliva, hair, or milk can give us a lot of information about our "body burden," the toxins and chemicals that accumulate in our bodies over time. Chemicals enter our bodies through what we devour, inhale, and gulp. Skin, our largest organ, is also permeable. It allows many chemicals we smother onto it to penetrate through its layers. Once inside, many chemicals pass right on through our system like a tourist, detected in our urine in a few short hours. Other chemicals seek out fatty tissues, like breast tissue, nestle in, and reside for decades. It's likely that all of us now live with some amount of body burden.

In 2004, the Environmental Working Group and Commonweal,* a nonprofit research and educational institute, conducted a body burden study. The findings were shared in a documentary titled *10 Americans* and was narrated by Ken Cook, the founder of the Environmental Working Group. Confident and amicable, Cook describes that through biomonitoring, samples of blood taken from ten Americans were analyzed for 413 chemicals. 287 chemicals were found in the blood samples—an average of two hundred chemicals per person—including the exiled PCBs.

The first time I viewed this presentation, I was angered. A banned chemical from the 1970s was still floating around inside these bodies? Yet these ten blood donors had not devoured food sprayed with pesticide, nor were they exposed to harsh cleaning products. They had never jumped into a lake laden with PCBs looking for a fishing pole or systematically applied layers of bug spray. The ten blood samples were taken from umbilical cords. Ten random samples from tiny humans born pre-polluted. Horrifyingly, the video breaks down the links to harm. Of the 212 chemicals:

- 134 had been shown to cause cancer
- 154 caused hormone disruption
- 186 were associated with infertility

....
* No, this is not a spelling error. Commonweal means "for the public good." It is also an amazing nonprofit health and environmental research institute in Bolinas, California, offering programs that contribute to human and ecosystem health.

- 130 were immune system toxicants
- 151 were associated with causing birth defects
- 158 were neurotoxins like lead, mercury, and PCBs

How many pregnant mothers spend an inordinate amount of time protectively avoiding peanut butter, shellfish, lunchmeat, and soft cheeses, all in the hopes of preventing potential food allergies or Listeria contamination from harming our perfectly innocent unborn babies? We pass down our eye color, the father's hair color, fingernail shape, and body type. We hope our new baby gets his grandmother's kind heart and passes over her grandfather's bowel troubles. What else are we passing onto our children?

How many chemicals have you saved up? What unwanted guests are you hosting? Most of us will never know, as biomonitoring isn't a widely available procedure and is very costly. What effects will we face from such accumulation? Do the toxins hibernate undetected in our systems since the womb and gain momentum over time? Do chemicals collected in utero interact and compound with those we collect during adolescence? Will they lead to infertility? Memory issues? Obesity? Cancer? These are the questions of our time. What we are uncovering blows my mind. Science may not be able to tell us exactly what causes problems we may experience, but we do know we are unravelling a tangled labyrinth of toxins within our body.

Does that mean my, or any, efforts are a waste of time? I'll just say it—is it too late? Are we screwed? Is succumbing to quicksand our only choice? No. No. No. PCBs and other persistent chemicals are here to haunt us, to deliver a message, much like a spirit straight from Charles Dickens' *A Christmas Carol*, foreboding, warning, "I am the Ghost of Christmas Present. Look upon me!" Now is the time to aggressively ban other known persistent and bioaccumulative chemicals, even if it will be a slow road until they are actually diminished. It is obvious we should have started these changes decades ago, but that doesn't mean we give up. Dickens' moral presses down, "But if the courses be departed from, the ends will change." Now is the time.

And a Little Bit of Grief

As promised, the Taxol replacing major chemotherapy treatments was less destructive to my body than its predecessor was. However, the slowly building side effects were sinister. Within weeks, my new norm was to function with constant, gnawing, bone pain. Lifting my purse made me wince from joint aches. I slid out of the car with the speed of a ninety-seven-year-old with arthritis. Soon, it hurt to turn over in my sleep. I tried to focus on the end goal and check off each week.

With the notorious chemos crossed off, I received less attention, leaving room for emotions to surface. I was exhausted, and my courage was slipping. I was tired of the whole stupid journey. My clipboard pointed out I was nowhere near the end of my list. Yet, shouldn't I be grateful? Look at what I had put behind me! Surgery! Chemo! I would have felt guilty whining to my husband and friends. They had spent months holding my life together, and now I wanted to bitch? What kind of ungrateful cancer survivor was I anyway? Instead, I crashed each evening, my husband continuing to be my rock and taking over where I left off in parenting. I was tired of being strong—physically and emotionally.

One evening, I retreated to where this mom goes for peace—my closet. Detesting the stupid knit hat I had been wearing, I yanked it off and flung it against a pile of duffle bags. Collapsing in the darkness, I grasped my bald head and grieved. The weak part of me took over. I hated everything. The why-me's, the I-hate-this, and the God-damnits erupted, followed by the desperation of oh-God-help-me's. My levee broke, and emotions flooded the closet floor. Curling around a heaping pile of dirty laundry, I pulled a sweatshirt to my face to muffle my shrieks and cries, while my family ate spaghetti far away downstairs. Ungracious, unthankful, what had I become? Inside, a tiny, guardian voice consoled, *This is part of the process. Let it out.*

It was okay to be me, doing this on the floor.

So I did. Sobs squeezed out until there were none left, and I lay there exhausted and limp, like a wrung-out washcloth.

Abruptly, the closet door opened, and light from my bedroom exposed my raw state to my daughter. Catapulted back to the present, my mind ripped into pieces. I tried to compose myself, but my grief had struck deep into her. Bewilderment, twisted with sadness and wise empathy, spread across her toddler face. Should I straighten myself? Pretend all was normal? I crawled over, pulled her up in my arms, and held her there in the partially lit closet amidst winter boots and folded sweaters. Snot and tears trickled into her hair. Four, five, ten minutes went by in silence.

Maternal voices, centuries old, reassured me that grieving was not exclusive to cancer. Mothers throughout time experienced devastation and emotional exhaustion, whether through divorce, trauma, or loss. We grieve, we cry, we blacken pillows with mascara as we muffle our sobs at night. We think no one is listening. When little souls outside the door hear, should we acknowledge their presence or brush them away? Do we reveal our private anguish and risk stealing bits of their inno-cence, or push on through lunches and carpools without explanation, our swollen eyelids the only clues we give away in the morning?

I adjusted my mother hat back into place and reassured her I was okay. Sometimes it feels good to cry. It is okay to let feelings out. I hugged her and told her I loved her. Inside, I felt horrible—worried this dread-ful experience would be ingrained in her memory, always a part of her.

Fatigue exposed my self-doubts. One would think knowledge of bioac-cumulation and biomonitoring would be the only arsenal I needed to ignite my emotions and continue on my quest with laser-like focus. But sometimes, doubt slithered into my mind. After tucking my kids in at night and removing foofy throw pillows from my bed, exhaustion har-assed, *What are you doing Kristi? Seriously, you wasted your day on this? Your friends think you are woo-woo, why are you driven to do this?* I tried to stomp on the thoughts telling me my priorities should be laundry, painting the dining room, or preparing for a cookie swap. If it wasn't insecurities, it was mother-guilt imploring; *Was I too preoccupied to hug my kids today? Did I laugh with them?*

When I am really lost and trying to find my place within environmental health, I shush the questioning with a tool. I flip back my comforter, march to my desk, and power up the computer. I rewatch the film *10 Americans*. Although I have seen it dozens of times, the ending always fuels my focus. My insecurities slowly morph into protective, maternal outrage.

Baby boomers were born into the synthetic chemical revolution. Now, revoltingly, babies were born chemically polluted. What better reason did I need to continue on this path? I started out to make my health a priority, but now my vision evolved into a broader mission. Decisions I made about the products I used affected not just the healthy glow of my skin but my community, my neighbors, and my grandchildren. I might not have understood why I was drawn to this subject, but I had no doubt it was what I was supposed to be doing. So what if my children learned a little early to make their own lunches and fold their own clothes? I considered it a step toward independence. The food in the pantry ran dangerously on empty. Frequently. It encouraged my children to be thankful when I did go grocery shopping. *10 Americans* was my tickling reminder to revel in my passion. Surrendering to this calling carried me to my next tour stop on my personal manifest destiny. Before I dumped my entire house into a rented garbage dumpster or abstained from purchasing anything ever again, I had a bit more groundwork to cover. Then, I could let the adventures begin.

Moonlighters

I confess. Ten years ago, I would scoff at any news flash sensationalizing a probable carcinogen. I'd think, *What doesn't cause cancer these days?* I had long given up questioning which viral emails—from soy food to used chopsticks to tanning beds—had threads of truth. Deleting them seemed simpler. I disregarded the casual manner with which the news anchors threw the noncommittal words "probably" and "possibly" around to describe cancer-causing agents. *Is it or isn't it?* These words fell into the family tree of "maybe" and "who knows." What I didn't understand was that these words were not ambiguous but were actual classification systems. Two separate programs responsible for most of the carcinogen classification references are the National Toxicology Program (NTP) and the International Agency for Research on Cancer (IARC). The NTP criteria use the terms: "Known to Be Human Carcinogen'" and "Reasonably Anticipated to be Human Carcinogen." The IARC, on the other hand, uses many more (and less direct) labels, which are:

- Carcinogenic to Humans
- Probably Carcinogenic to Humans
- Possibly Carcinogenic to Humans
- Not Classifiable as to Carcinogenicity in Humans
- Probably not Carcinogenic to Humans

In addition to these labels, the EPA or individual states may also create their own classification system. The California Environmental Protection Agency (CalEPA) has its own list of "chemicals known to the state to cause cancer or reproductive toxicity."

To me, these labels fall into the spectrum of everything from "causes cancer," to "we don't know if it's toxic," to "we hope it's not toxic." Not exactly the reassurance I need when I'm trying to figure out what lotion to smear on my toddler or what cleaning product to use on the floors my pets lick. Do you notice how none of the labels say, "Not a snowball's chance in hell it is carcinogenic" or "We pinky-swear it's not carcinogenic" or "100% proven to be safe, or we'll pay your medical bills?"

Even after their toxic properties are recognized, many chemicals stay in use. The true personalities of benzene, coal tar, vinyl chloride, and formaldehyde, are now categorized as "known to be human carcinogens" by the National Toxicology Program, yet they still cushion our daily life.

I have now modified my mindset and take warnings seriously. If an ingredient from an adhesive, paint thinner, cleaning product, or

what-have-you, makes the who's-who list of carcinogens, that's enough
for me. With health as my priority, I don't squander time evaluating the
nuances of a news anchor's warnings, but ask myself, "What can I do?
How can I reduce my exposure?" While I stand ready to pulverize carcinogens with the heel of my boot like a stained cigarette butt, an odd
fascination rises in me when learning about another term: endocrine
disrupting compounds.

If I could get a degree in "Home Eco-Momics 101," I would major in
Domestic Environmental Health, and my specialty would be endocrine
disruptors—chemicals that change the body's natural hormonal bal-
ances. For decades, these twisted toxin characters lived silently among
us, until their deceptive personalities were spotlighted in 1997 by
John Peterson Myers, Theo Colborn, and Dianne Dumanoski in their
groundbreaking book, *Our Stolen Future*. Since then, they have become
quite the hot topic, as each year we learn more about how and where
these disruptors operate.

Most endocrine disrupting compounds (EDCs) are chemicals initially designed with a specific function—such as an antifungal in cosmetics, as building blocks in polycarbonate plastic, or as a plastic softener.
They are commonly found in automobiles, baby care products, cleaning
materials, food packaging, pesticides, insecticides, and flame-retard-
ants, to name a few. The problem is, they do not always stay put but
sometimes leach out and end up in our bodies. Once inside, our systems
do not perceive them as wayward product ingredients but as additional
hormones like estrogen, progesterone, and testosterone. They can also
block normal hormone function.*

My endocrine disruptor studies were under the mentoring of the
Breast Cancer Fund. I loved their user-friendly website and enrolled in
several conference calls during which I sat quietly learning from activists and educators from around the world. I advanced from freshman

---

* Hormones behave as chemical messengers, transporting signals from one cell to another,
regulating phenomenal functions such as how our reproductive organs develop, how our bodies
metabolize food, and how our pancreas reacts to sugars.

to sophomore endocrine disruptor studies, soaking in what made them unique. EDCs flip the traditional notion that the "dose makes the poison" or the greater the dose, the more toxic to the body. Even small amounts of these disruptors are dangerous to our systems. I had heard manufacturers pacify fears by assuring consumers that a questionable ingredient existed in their product in "trace amounts" or even parts per billion. I used to reassure myself with quippy sayings like "everything in moderation" to justify warnings. It was my excuse to indulge. Now we know endocrine disruptors can be terribly impactful *because of* their small dose. Imagine your body gagging on an accidental swig of sour milk. You know something isn't right with the milk, but you swallow it anyway. The message from the smell might hit your brain, your throat may tighten, and you might run over to the sink to force it out. Our bodies react sometimes violently, possibly shutting down functions or trying to purge doses of something it determines to be toxic. To protect. To survive. However, endocrine disrupting compounds do not enter the body through gulps or large doses but subtly, as miniscule trespassers. They are able to interact inside us without sounding off alarms. The Breast Cancer Fund describes sophisticated endocrine disruptors as creating devastating effects at infinitesimally small levels of exposure, especially during early critical windows of vulnerability.[33]

I used my Breast Cancer Fund *State of the Evidence* report as a resource—the one marked with yellow and blue Sharpie shorthand, scribbled thoughts, and an accidental smear of butternut squash chili. The Breast Cancer Fund states, "Total exposures to estrogens, estrogen mimickers, and endocrine system disruptors—from any number of sources—have been associated with increased risk for breast cancer later in life."[34] Rather than looking for single, direct causes, the Fund encourages us to recognize that there are multiple, interacting factors that influence risk. My children crawling on the kitchen floor may encounter the endocrine disruptors alkylphenol and dibutyl phthalate from cleaning products. A pregnant woman eating strawberries while commuting in traffic might encounter atrazine, dioxins, and trichloroethylene. Multiple exposures, multiple sources, with variations of vulnerability.

We have come a long way. Our ability to manipulate chemicals at trace amounts has resulted in some magnificent feats. I can elect to wear a birth control patch—a thin, adhesive, two inch square paper on my arm—and have it alter my reproductive functions dramatically. The infinitesimal amount of hormones on the sticker has the power to thicken my cervical mucus, change my endometrium, and prevent ovulation. We like the freedom trace amounts of chemicals afford us. It makes life easier, despite side effects. We're willing to eat "light" potato chips containing the same synthetic oil currently used in deck stain and as a power tool lubricant, even though it prevents the absorption of vitamins and can cause bloating and stomach cramps. Have we crossed a line of caution to where chemicals can manipulate us without our knowledge?

Rigorous research is needed to continue to understand how endocrine disruptors are implicated in interfering with our hormone-driven processes. We need to understand why breast development and menstruation in our daughters is occurring at a much younger age. Or how other disruptors are suspect in interfering with metabolism and contributing to obesity. How everyday endocrine disrupting compounds may interfere with the performance of certain chemotherapy agents. It is easier to place blame on singular causes—like tobacco causing lung cancer. We need to shift our thinking and understand that multiple exposures from many different types of chemicals are just as dangerous; it isn't always the dose that makes the poison. It's possible to change our thinking; we have adjusted our mindsets before. Christopher Columbus proved the world wasn't flat. Until Nicolaus Copernicus cleared our confusion, we believed Earth was the center of the solar system. It may very well be that endocrine disruptors are this generation's frontier to be conquered.

Toxic Stew

Following the nearby college's manicured and curving sidewalks, I pushed through my morning power walk. With exaggerated arm-pumping motion, I ruminated—trying to separate facts from feelings. I needed to purge, file, and organize my mind. All the information gathered in my brain was like a hoarder's home with no room to move. I decided to stick with that method employed in those home-organizing books and made a cranial file for three categories: keep, give away, and throw away. I needed to pack emotion in the throwaway file (who was going to listen to me if I was ranting with angst and dismay?), extra information in the give-away-file (surely someone else could benefit from all this data, Salvation Army perhaps?), and place only what was relevant to my mission in the keep-file. Deciding what to keep and what to trash was difficult. I now had a new appreciation for those over-collecting people who cry and refuse to give up their peeling gold trophy or their hair scrunchie collection from the 90s.

I started by addressing my emotions. I knew synthetic chemicals had many positive contributions. Undeniably, they extended life spans, eradicated diseases, and saved lives—hopefully mine included. I'll admit it, the overwhelmingness of it all brought fleeting thoughts of desperation. I wanted to time travel to 1860, to an untainted, virgin parcel of land in the mountain ranges of Montana where I could raise my children, sheltered and protected. Revelling in Western romance, I pictured hitching up horses to my covered wagon and following the setting sun westward. We would sleep under the stars, cook our meals over a campfire, and chase jackrabbits for entertainment. My kids would fish, climb oak trees, and swim in any pond they wanted. Sensibility pointed out there would be drawbacks to this plan. First, there would likely be no central heat. My Wyoming-raised husband tells me that Rocky Mountain state winters are a bit chilly. There would not be an army of washing machines, dryers, or dishwashers ready to work with the push of my fingertip. No refrigerator to keep my frozen fish sticks cold. I realized I would be left with a Ma-Ingalls list of domestic chores, which I am not particularly adept at or fond of. Most importantly, there would be no flushing toilet. I'm really pretty attached to flushing toilets. My emotions were a nice place to hide for a time, but abandoning conveniences was reactionary. With my daydreams and magazine clippings, I fantasized about the interior of my cabin in Montana, but that was not the solution. While I couldn't escape, I could start to influence the one-acre we inhabited. I could have an impact within my own home, on my own body, and in my children's lives while they lived with me, right here in our colonial home in a suburb in Massachusetts.

I stopped my powerwalk, pulled out my ear buds, and placed my hands on my hips. A know-it-all voice judiciously corrected, *Not all harmful chemicals are synthetic.* Mercury, radon, and lead, are some examples of chemicals that occur naturally in our world, manufactured by Mother Nature herself. Mercury compounds could be found in eye drops and in mascara under the name thimerosal. Recklessly disposing of thermometers and curlicue CFL light bulbs can leach mercury into our soil and water, possibly damaging our brains and nervous systems. Radon, another naturally occurring gas in the soil, is responsible for an estimated twenty thousand lung cancer deaths each year. Many people are familiar with the dangers of lead in paint and the poisoning symptoms including memory loss, mood swings, and joint and muscle disorders.[35] The United States has taken actions to reduce exposure to lead since the 1970s; yet in 2009, FDA studies found lead as a common contaminant in lipstick.[36]

Picking up my pace again, ear buds in place, the debate did not boil down to whether toxins were human-designed or occurred naturally in the environment. Not all toxins were synthetic. It was the links to harm, the abundance, and the complexity that concerned me. I furrowed my eyebrows, pursed my lips, and tightened my core, creating the silly but effective power-walk-waddle. I was almost at the end of my workout. Keep pushing. Don't give up. Emotions were aside. One hundred and fifty years of history had brought me back to the same driving point—the grain of sand—that the constant applications and complex inter-actions of products containing harmful ingredients was what bothered me. The repeated, cumulative, and interacting exposures. A daily sim-mering toxic stew.

Back at my car, I opened the driver's side door, unzipped my sweat-shirt, and gulped cold water. Before a congressional committee and in *Silent Spring,* Rachel Carson asserted that one of the most basic rights must surely be the "right of the citizen to be secure in his own home against the intrusion of poisons applied by other persons."[37] Each time I recited this statement, chills moved through me. Fifty years have passed since the publication of her landmark book, yet her plea is as relevant today as it was then. I was dispirited by our human behavior and blind use of dangerous chemicals when we had the seeds of knowl-edge so long ago. The fifty-year anniversary of *Silent Spring* would be in 2012. It was time to make a radical impact on my health, on my family, and on my children. On my one-day grandchildren. If Carson could accomplish so much in her lifetime—inspiring the government, chal-lenging large chemical companies, and igniting our society when there was no green movement, no product alternatives, and very few people listening—what could I accomplish in my home with those benefits at my disposal?

I laughed aloud when I thought about my previous attempt to compile a cheat sheet of chemicals. What an ultimate fail! I had started by trying to list the most toxic ingredients first, but the lack of data frustrated me. I then switched to a Word table listing twelve of the most common ingredients I could find. This quickly expanded to my "tainted twenty." Fifteen pages later, I abandoned this task entirely. I tried printing little wallet cards for easy reference when shopping but questioned where I was supposed to draw the line of what was considered a "common" ingredient. Some exposures were daily and some were seasonal. None of this was enjoyable or productive. It was a downer, distracting me from focusing. I tried. I really did. Searching the back of every single item in my shopping cart did not make me a happy mother (or woman). It was unrealistic. Nobody else was going to do this. If I wanted to be successful in my new health endeavor, I needed to change my approach. My methods would have to be simple to implement, not require a lot of time, and be budget conscious.

Stepping out of list-making mode, instead of tackling suspicious characters one-by-one, I reduced my efforts to focus on three areas in which I could make little changes and choose wiser:

> Products with which we **smother** our skin.
> Foods we **devour**.
> Surroundings in which we **immerse** ourselves.

Smother

"If someone were to ask you, 'What's that lovely fragrance you're wearing?' would you say, 'Oh, those are hormone disruptors, allergens, and chemicals that have never been assessed for safety. It's my signature scent.' Of course you wouldn't. But there is a good chance that reply would be accurate."

~Mia Davis, Campaign for Safe Cosmetics

Foundation

Armed with inspiration, vocabulary, and fresh revelations, I was craving to actually make an impact. Strategically, I chose a small area as my starting point: the bathroom closet. It seemed easier to begin with a project I knew I could finish in a relatively short amount of time, which I figured would give me motivation to overhaul another cupboard. Or even another closet. If I tried to tackle, say, every product that touched my skin from makeup to laundry soap, I knew I would feel overwhelmed and be tempted to give up. Purging the cozy bathroom closet was my best bet.

I eagerly tugged open the white double doors and let my eyes roam over the shelves. *This shouldn't be too hard,* I reassured myself. After all, I really didn't wear much makeup. In front of me, a disheveled accumulation of bottles, applicators, and lotions shared space with boxes of bulk-purchased toothpaste. Should I include all personal care products or just cosmetics? Should I focus on my husband's products too? Would he appreciate that, or even notice? His shelf had a different collection of shampoo, deodorant, shaving cream, soap, and toothpaste. Eventually I wanted to evaluate my family's products too. Selfishly, a feeling of accomplishment beckoned, and I settled on just my own routine.

I started in the left corner of my shelf and reviewed the stockpile. A blue, plastic tackle box stored a cache of liquid and cream foundations in shades ranging from buff to ivory. The tones and variety of brands reflected my ongoing struggle to match the cool undertone of my jaw line to the warm freckles on my cheeks. I was embarrassed to spot a foundation-stained triangle foam applicator that had sat there for who knows how long. Tucked next to the tackle box was a shoebox (toddler's size-twelve winter boot) containing an 80s-like collection of purple and bronze eye shadows. Fingering the plastic compacts, I mused, *When was the last time I used these?* No doubt when I was on a quest to achieve a sultry "smoky eye" or "naturally" radiant summer glow. The dozen lipsticks next to the box however, well, those were different. Lipstick was my daily-coveted habit; I was not the same without it. If I skipped applying some shade of raspberry on my pallid lips, I risked concerned comments from family. "Are you feeling well? You look kinda pale." A quick smear of waxy Revlon in the morning and I was magically transformed into robust health. Lipstick was my one must-have, go-to beauty product. For years, I collected them like shells on the beach, enamored by their many colors and finishes—matte, glossy, indelible. I rolled my lipstick friends around and chuckled at shades I purchased knowing they'd never look good on me. Well, when a product bears an orange clearance sticker, what's a girl to do? Even ugly colors deserve at least a shot.

Moving along, I reached toward the back and grabbed the hair-styling containers. It had been over a year now since I needed hair products; my collection sat unloved beneath a layer of dust. Mousse for scrunching. Gel for sleeking. Conditioners bought under buy-one, get-one-half-off deals. Expensive pomade for sculpting flippy-dos that only flopped. How much had I saved this past year without hair? I turned toward the mirror and ran my fingers through my ultra-short layers. Feeling a little bad ass and channeling my inner Joan Jett, I squirted a dollop of gel into my hand and spiked my boy cut. Tilting my head, I smiled at the fuzzy undergrowth of hair filling in along my scalp. The excitement of this hair growth was offset by the fact that my scalp had filled in starting at the back. However, the bangs, for whatever reason, were torturously taking their time. Just like a newborn. This cruel order of growth bitterly required haircuts; otherwise, a Billy Ray mullet would replace my Joan Jett spikes in no time.

I pushed aside the hair products and endeavored to untangle another box containing a mess of black electrical cords. Over the years, I had accumulated quite the collection of curling irons: black and silver, fat barreled, skinny barreled, and the stupid, spiral curling iron that never worked. I even found my old crimper; although looking back, I am not sure why I felt the need to go with a hairstyle reminiscent of being electrocuted. Completing my hair appliance collection was a set of hot rollers, you know, for those big, bouncy, natural looking curls. Running my fingers down a svelte, glass perfume bottle, its signature shape reminded me of days courting my husband. The bottle had been empty for ages, but nostalgia wouldn't let me throw it away, so it lived here among other intoxicating Christmas-gift perfumes.

I shook my head. All this junk displayed before me was making me twitch. What if I just took some time to purge? Took a day or two before I started looking for hidden chemicals and reorganized the bathroom instead? It could even use a coat of paint. Maybe I should start there. I was easily being sidetracked from my purpose, which was to identify any unhealthy beauty products and get rid of them. I'd worry about replacing them later. *Focus,* I told myself. *You can do this.*

One more box beckoned. Nine nail polishes falling within a narrow spectrum of Shimmering Rose to Wine Rose to Raspberry Rose lined a second shoebox (size seven women's aerobic) along with cotton balls, acrid polish remover, and a rarely-used toe-spreading pedicure tool. Two nail polishes with gummed lids patiently waited for the day I would break out the pliers and forcefully unseal them. As I rummaged, I remembered the first community workshop I attended had warned of nail polishes containing formaldehyde and two other ingredients. Certainly we didn't brush ingredients onto our nail beds that induced cancer in rats, did we? Wouldn't a company have to disclose that on the polish bottles if it were true? Still, I was intrigued. Could I tackle just this shoebox of polish today? That seemed feasible. Sliding the victim-box off the shelf, I noticed the towel pile needed straightening and there were globs of toothpaste in the sink I really should scrape up...I brushed those thoughts out of my mind and bumped the bathroom door closed with my hip.

I set the rectangular box on my desk as if it were a container of hazardous materials and quickly calculated how much time I had until the first bus pick-up. Fifty-three minutes. Where to start, where to start? What was the goal here? Simple, really. To find out if the polish I used contained harmful chemicals. Maybe the Toxic Substance Control Act website and its eighty-some thousand registered ingredients would provide direction. Clicking from link to link, I was surprised to discover TSCA didn't classify or regulate cosmetics. Slight detour, but the school bus would arrive soon so I pressed on.

I tapped my fingers on the desk. If TSCA didn't regulate cosmetics, who did? Why didn't I know this? After all, hadn't I been a training manager at Garden Botanika? I used to translate the benefits of calendula, chamomile, and jojoba into sales techniques for the makeup and skin care retail chain. Under my instruction, nineteen-year-old sales associates blossomed, armed with knowledge of Elder Flower Toning Lotion and Sweet Almond Oil. What could I pull from my past to assist me? I knew any product trolling to clinch the sale could embellish the label with the word *organic*, regardless of the concoction inside. The words *organic, earth-friendly, natural*—even directly in the name of the product—had no legal definition. To confuse the matter more, I knew the United States had its own certified organic program for cosmetics, but this covered ingredients grown in agriculture, not the ones raised in test tubes. It certainly didn't assess the safety of synthetic products. This was important but not exactly what I was looking for.

My personal research assistant, Ms. Google, offered sensible answers: our very own Food and Drug Administration (FDA). Of course. I rolled my chair forward, only to discover the legislation "regulating" cosmetics was the Food, Drug, and Cosmetic Act of 1938. This act went into effect before the trendy mass use of hand sanitizers, tanning crème, mineral makeup, suntan lotion, and hair straighteners.*[38] Yet, it was under the FDC Act that the Cosmetic Ingredient Review (CIR) panel was created to determine the safety of personal care products.

While I had originally been thankful for the CIR panel's efforts to attempt to create safety assessments, I later learned that under this system, lead is allowed in lipsticks and formaldehyde in baby shampoo.† The industry-funded CIR panel had only reviewed eleven percent of all ingredients in cosmetics, finding only nine of the ingredients tested

....

* A National Public Radio story added a nice twist to my perspective with a story on shampoo. In 1908, the New York Times advised women it was okay to wash their hair every two weeks from the usual monthly norm. Can you imagine? It wasn't until the inundation of marketing in the 1970s that daily washing became the norm. Think how much time I could save....

† A jaw-dropping one in five personal care products contain chemicals linked to cancer, and eighty percent contain ingredients that commonly contain hazardous impurities. If that weren't crazy enough, fifty-six percent contain penetration enhancers that actually help deliver ingredients deeper into the skin!

unsafe. As I mentioned earlier, this is in comparison to the European Union's Cosmetic Directive, which has banned eleven hundred possible ingredients. Scrolling through the CIR panel's website, there were many ingredients categorized from "safe-as used" to "insufficient data," but where could I turn for regulations to ensure that what I was dabbing and brushing on my body was tested and monitored for long-term health effects? And what about combining products? Did ingredients I layered on my skin interact with each other? Did my bar soap mix with my body lotion and mix again with my perfume and hairspray to create some sort of toxic stew? I could find nothing to help me understand the totality of products when I used them together in my beauty routine.

I slumped in my chair. This was crazy. The nail polish soldiers in the box next to me stood at attention with smug, "gotcha" looks. The manufacturer of my nail polish—or any personal care product—could use any ingredient the company determined was safe. I was puzzled. That's a little bit like allowing a four-year-old to choose her breakfast. If it were up to my chocolate-loving daughter, brownies would be healthy morning fare. After all, they do contain eggs, flour, and oil, just like pancakes and muffins. But I disagree. I have higher standards for her body and mine. Just because a company claims something is safe doesn't make it so. For me, the dispute seemed to hinge around the definition of "safe." The CIR panel standards are different from those I find acceptable for my body. What was perceived safe when I worked in the industry in the late 1990s no longer applies. Our use of chemicals has changed so much in twenty years, how can I rely on a document from 1938? I just can't. The Cosmetic Industry Review panel can declare something as "safe," and society can cry "not safe enough." Of course, only if we know about it.

Before I clicked out of my online search session, I found this confounding and ludicrous recommendation by the FDA: "testing laboratories were listed in the telephone directory."[39] Right. I was going to take all my stuffed shoe boxes down to the local testing laboratory and have them tested for safety, right in between karate lessons and making stir-fry. I bet it's affordable, all that laboratory testing, considering that the last time I had a urinalysis, a single test alone was a thirty-five dollar co-pay. Nevertheless, the message from the FDA couldn't be clearer: figuring out if a product was "safe" was up to me, a real-life example of caveat emptor—buyer beware. Beware indeed.

I pulled out a rounded bottle of polish and painted my thumbnail with Plum Rose in three meticulous strokes. My Nana taught me the art of applying polish without staining my cuticles when I was eight. Never did she whisper in my ear that it was up to me to decide if the product was safe enough. I was frustrated. I blew air on my paint job, twisted on the lid, and rolled the bottle around in my hand. Staring right at me in the tiniest of eye-squinting fonts was the nasty trio I had been warned to stay away from: formaldehyde, dibutyl phthalate, and toluene. One, two, and three. Damn. Are you kidding me? Well, at least I had a spelling reference and could search for those items on the Internet.

Clicking on the Women's Voices for the Earth website, I finally began to learn about these three chemicals:

- Toluene prevents the nail polish from separating in the bottle and allows for a smooth finish. The fumes from nail polish contain a "volatile solvent" which cause eye, throat, and lung irritation and can affect the central nervous system.
- Formaldehyde helps the nail polish harden and evaporates into the air. Formaldehyde is known to cause cancer.
- Dibutyl phthalate (DBP), a plasticizing chemical, helps the nail polish remain flexible and shiny. Exposure to this chemical can "affect thyroid function and in pregnant women has been linked to reproductive problems in baby boys as well as to decreased sperm count in adult men."[40]

These three ingredients were added to the nail polish for specific purposes: to make the polish shiny, more elastic, and to elongate the shelf life of the product. But those chemicals also leeched out into our environment and into our permeable nail beds, potentially disrupting our systems. The question left now was, could nail polish be manufactured without these ingredients, or would I have to give up manis and pedis for the rest of my life? Turns out, there were plenty of alternatives proudly boasting they were "three-free," meaning free of toluene, formaldehyde, and DBP. As I started to shop around, I spotted "three-free" on some brands and became giddy after I inspected the base of the bottle and discovered the ingredients were absent. The best part? They were just as pretty, just as effective, and just as affordable as the tainted brands.

Trio of Tools

Understanding my nail polish was a tiny triumph that fueled my quest for continued purging. During this time, three more tools materialized: one pioneering database, two fellow students, and an investigative book. With these tools and to the best of my consumer-ability, I gave my bathroom an extreme makeover, box by box.

At the same time I was rebuilding my body, the Environmental Working Group (EWG) was preparing to unveil the Skin Deep Cosmetic Database. The first of its kind, this database merged personal care products with public toxicity and regulatory databases. This meant consumers could learn about the safety and toxicity of almost 65,000 products with over 7,000 ingredients. (This site currently receives roughly a million views a month, and no, not all are mine.)

I dumped my daughter's sparkly lip-gloss collection onto my desk, adding to the growing pile of products I wanted to know more about. I decided to employ my Halloween candy sorting method to filter through products while using the Skin Deep Cosmetic Database. The "Green Light" pile to my left would be products I would keep (the wrapped candies). The "Yellow Light" pile directly in front of me consisted of products I either couldn't find a green option for or would use up first and then replace (the homemade foodstuffs from neighbors, wrapped, but still suspect). The third group to my right, the "Red Light" pile, were for items linked to harmful ingredients (the legendary, cyanide-laced pixie sticks and razor-filled apple group). My kids had been safely eating Halloween candy for years using this same process, and it was one I was familiar with. This method turned out to be a good decision on my part, as the Database also used the green-yellow-red light method to rate products.

I keyed the brand names of the products into the Database, hoping, of course, to find all green lights. That wasn't the case however. I was dismayed to find that a couple of my daughter's lip-glosses earned a yellow or red light. I sorted the cosmetics into my various piles, clucking with maternal disappointment at the third pile. Someone at these companies actually filled these products with ingredients known to cause harm. Did they consciously spike the punch like a teenager at prom, or were they unaware of their actions and simply doing their job? Regardless, I decided I would not purchase these products again and placed a sour note in my mental rolodex.

Sadly, a fourth pile grew faster than a heap of laundry after a camping trip. This pile accumulated under the category "lack of data." The Environmental Working Group explained, "Many ingredients don't have publicly available information, therefore can't be compared. Ninety percent of ingredients have not been assessed for safety even by the industry's own safety panel."[41] This growing pile made it clear to me that there was a need for a system that shared information among all manufacturers and consumers, along with a need for more testing.

I did appreciate that with a few keystrokes, I could start a relationship with a foreign ingredient in the Database. When researching my nail polishes, three clicks of the mouse told me everything I wanted to know about toluene. The page displayed toluene as a "Red 10" with twelve alias names, seventy-five products it is known to be used in, and references indicating toluene has "strong evidence as a human developmental and nervous system toxicant."

While the Skin Deep Database clearly wasn't going to be my one-stop-shop for answers, it was a great place to begin and more than I had before—something is always better than nothing. As I ran low on a product, I would enter the category (such as shampoo, lotion, or hairspray) into the Skin Deep Database. I'd scroll down and scan for familiar brands. Then I would open a second window on my computer screen to check prices on the Target and Vitacost websites. Finally, I transferred the product to my grocery list for the following week's errands. Nice and neat.

While the Skin Deep Database offered me the science of a particular ingredient, it didn't compare to the motivation I found taking this journey arm-in-arm with my two girlfriends. Tara and Karen were my gal pals who had joined me at the community workshop. As fellow students, we commiserated together about our attempts to find the right shampoo, sunscreen, and deodorant. We jubilantly texted each other when we found deals on green-ranked products while shopping. We were collectively perplexed when we learned about yet another country banning an ingredient we used daily. Together, we gradually challenged ourselves to raise the bar on each successive decision and figure out if wiser options existed. We watched our purchasing habits adapt as we selected simpler and used less.

I met Tara when her son was in my Cub Scout troop. She's tall and slender; her naturally curly hair cascades in wisps and spirals. She has an incredibly perceptive mind with a knack for details. If she had a question about a product, she tenaciously researched websites and sent inquiries to companies on a quest for answers. She often received replies, sometimes with coupons. Tara investigated her personal products one by one and gave her surroundings a Home Eco-Momics makeover. With her as my role model, I slowly stopped being a passive consumer and contacted companies as well. I started taking thirty seconds out of my day to send an encouraging email to companies who were leading the way by doing the right thing, to let them know I appreciated the options they provided. I also sent emails to companies of which I had been a lifelong customer but now decided there were better options. I let them know I was breaking up with them, dumping their old-school ways for the young, sensitive version I craved. Maybe my email ended up filling the trash at headquarters, but maybe not. Perhaps if they received many letters over time, they would change their ways. Tara set the bar for me, and I followed her admirable lead.

My friendship with Karen was founded on proximity; she lives next door. As neighbors, we have celebrated puppies, pregnancies, first days of school, and endless carpools. Her delicate features and tiny frame contain a deeply loyal, generous soul. Fed up with what she found in the marketplace, she decided to opt out from these products entirely and not rely on the self-regulated industries' definition of safety. Instead, she researched healthy ingredients to make body care products for her three daughters. She created effective, loving recipes for makeup removers, scrubs, and lotions using mainly organic ingredients. I envied her patience and drive. After offering her products to friends and family, Karen dedicated her passion to natural and toxin-free bath and body products, entrepreneurial style, and established Be Green Bath and Body. Karen shares with clients: "What I desired was a simple, healthy, natural way to nourish my skin. I set out to read everything I could about natural ingredients. I spent months researching green skin care and formulating 100% natural, toxin-free beauty products. That is how Be Green Bath and Body was born."

It was a privilege to witness the birth of a business and listen to the decisions she had to face. Choices in ingredients, packaging, and price could have made her business explode in size, but inevitably, she always chose in the name of quality and steady growth, believing in her strong desire to share safe and healthy skin care with others.

While my frustration peaked at wanting to accomplish everything at once, Karen had the gift of enjoying the journey. She loved to create the more challenging products—day creams and body lotions—tweaking and working batches of day cream until she accomplished the perfect consistency. Even though it was labor intensive, she loved investing time trying to understand emulsions (mixing oils and water), feeling proud that she could do it. Because of her, I started to shop differently. When I'd lean on the cart while inspecting a prospective product, my mind would flash to Karen. She was making equally effective products at home in her blender. I questioned, *What was I about to pay for?* The upscale name? The layers of glitzy packaging? The expensive advertising? The CEO's bonuses and beachfront vacation home? Then, I'd gently return the product to its shelf and move onward.

While I hid behind a keyboard, Karen whipped up fresh batches of product to nourish her clients safely. On her refrigerator was a map where she colored in states as a small celebration of where she had shipped her products. With recent orders, I think she needs to get a globe instead.

At the start of all this, we were three individuals with our own interests and agendas. Maybe my cancer started the ball rolling, but Karen and Tara were the ones who kept it moving with me; each of us kicking it back and forth down the street, encouraging each other to kick it farther and faster than last time. Our combined personalities and strengths electrified my learning curve. Squeezed between life's activities and depressing cancer talk, we encouraged and confided in each other through flying emails and texts.

> *From:*   *Kristi*
> *To:*   *Tara, Karen*
> *Sent:*   *Tuesday, April 12 6:09 AM*
> *Omg. I so do not like this shampoo. Arrgh! My hair feels like dreadlocks in the making! Help me! It was a yellow on the Database and a decent price, but it did not pass the usage test!*

> *From:*   *Tara*
> *To:*   *Kristi, Karen*
> *Sent:*   *Tuesday, April 12 6:47 AM*
>
> *LOL. Which one did you try? Shampoos are hit or miss. I'm still searching.*
> *PS. Karen, LOVE, LOVE, LOVE the day cream! I wouldn't change a thing about it!*

From: *Karen*
To: *Kristi, Tara*
Sent: *Tuesday, April 12 1:32 PM*

Try using diluted cider vinegar and water to rinse your hair.
My sister gave me a book last week — Not Just a Pretty Face. It's very interesting. Have you read it?

From: *Kristi*
To: *Tara, Karen*
Sent: *Tuesday, April 12 2:52 PM*

Thank you thank you thank you. The cider vinegar solution did the trick. My hair is soft and clean.
Ahhh. Now off to two karate lessons and one ballet class. Karen, can I borrow the book? I have appointments at Dana Farber next week. That would be perfect. I'll pick it up at carpool?

From: *Tara*
To: *Kristi, Karen*
Sent: *Tuesday, April 12 7:50 PM*

Speaking of shampoo, I'm placing an order on Vitacost tomorrow. Do you need anything? Split the shipping cost?
Kristi, do you need coverage for the kids while you're at Dana-Farber? I can run Kyle over to guitar. Is everything ok?

```
From:      Kristi
To:        Tara, Karen
Sent:      Tuesday, April 12 9:59 PM
```

I'll pass on this Vitacost order. Going to Whole Foods this week to explore.

I'm all good on the kid coverage—and everything is fine (hugs). This appt. is a consultation for an oophorectomy. The docs are recommending I have my ovaries removed. What does that have to do with my rack you ask? Okay, so removing the ovaries will reduce hormones produced in my body, reducing chances of recurrence. It's my choice, and I'm leaning toward monthly shots over the surgery. Shots would only take a chunk of my day once a month and a surgery would be one more for my family to work around. They have never complained, but I hate this being their life, ya know?

As I returned a child's forgotten Cape Cod hoodie to Karen, she loaned me her copy of *Not Just a Pretty Face, The Ugly Side of the Beauty Industry,* by Stacy Malkan. When it came to doctor appointments, I had gone from foot-wiggling impatience to treasuring the lobby waiting time. In my blue plaid, tote bag, I carried everything from books to Christmas cards, taking advantage of the quiet time. I escaped into *Not Just a Pretty Face,* and became immediately engrossed in the story. When the receptionist called my name, it took all my strength to resist giving my appointment slot to the napping man next to me, so I could continue reading. With her investigative writing, Malkan carried me from the end of my timeline to present day. I had started my research in the late 1800s and traveled through the World Wars. *Silent Spring* catapulted me from the 1960s and dropped me into Generation X. Now, Stacy Malkan's book fused the personal care products industry directly into the environmental health movement.

While Everyday-Me's purged shelves and prodded companies to evolve, Stacy Malkan co-founded the Campaign for Safe Cosmetics.* Established in 2004, the Campaign has become our national voice and works to protect consumers and create change at the federal level. While I dumped shoeboxes of *slightly risky* and *practically nontoxic* crap from my three-foot bathroom shelf, the Campaign for Safe Cosmetics had been making a presence in the industry, influencing the removal of harmful ingredients. Their sisterly guidance comforted me, and I no longer felt the weight of being a sole protector on my shoulders. Finding the Campaign transformed me from a rogue woman on a quest to part of a movement—one that was pushing to eliminate dangerous chemicals from personal care products not just for myself, but for all men, women, and children.

I ran my eyes down the list of supporting organizations in the back of Malkan's book, and my perspective broadened. I was blown away by how many people were already on board and behind this movement. To stay connected, I started to volunteer at Campaign events where once again, I learned much more than I contributed. I admired advocates whose interests went beyond my self-centered breast cancer journey. I met and observed leaders who joined the Campaign to represent concerns such as autism, endometriosis, and fibromyalgia. Supporters of the Campaign included parents of children with asthma and couples struggling with reproductive issues; teachers and nurses; advocates for children with learning disorders. All rallied and supported the Campaign. I watched teenagers stage protests and pediatricians provide testimony. It was like discovering an underground dance club filled with people like me—people who were working and fighting for our right to health. I realized this was not just a stay-at-home mom's focus, and I was honored to join the tribe.

....
* Organizations across the country form the Campaign for Safe Cosmetics including the Breast Cancer Fund, Environmental Working Group, Women's Voices for the Earth, the Massachusetts Breast Cancer Coalition, Commonweal, The Alliance for a Healthy Tomorrow, Clean Water Action, National Black Environmental Justice Network, National Environmental Trust, and Friends for the Earth.

Two Mug Shots

Armed with my small arsenal—Skin Deep Database, girlfriends, and research tools—I was ready to educate myself on two offenders: parabens and phthalates. I had seen these words on labels, in magazine articles, and in newspaper reports defining the buzzwords. Wording on products claimed "phthalate free" or "paraben free" hinting I should avoid them, yet I didn't know why.

Turns out, there is more than one type of paraben. To help myself remember them, I referred to these offenders (methylparaben, ethylparaben, butylparaben, and propylparaben) as the hard-working paraben sisters. These multi-tasking career chemicals are commonly used as an antimicrobial in personal care products, allowing the product to last longer on store shelves. They are also considered estrogen mimickers, absorbed through skin and from the gastrointestinal tract and blood, and are found in almost all urine samples of adults in the United States. [42]

Many companies have been phasing out the use of parabens, replacing them with kinder preservatives. Karen explained, "In any kind of product where water is involved, like lotions and creams, it is important to use preservatives. I don't think synthetic preservatives are necessary. There are other things you can use. Honey, for instance, is a great preservative, not only for moisturizing your skin, but it also has antibacterial and antifungal qualities. Cinnamon, lemon and orange oils, and even fermented radish root are great to have in your products."

If parabens are the multi-tasking sisters, phthalates (pronounced thal-lates) have gained a reputation for being the bad boys as they are linked to harm, including reduced sperm counts and testicular atrophy in male test animals.[43] Phthalates are often used in plastics and cosmetics and are considered endocrine disruptors.

Sneaky little buggers, sometimes they hide from the most well-intentioned savvy consumer. While you might not find the term *phthalate* in the ingredient list on the back of a household product, if it says *fragrance*, phthalates could likely be hiding within. *Fragrance* is a catchall term for hundreds of possible ingredients, including phthalates. The cosmetic industry refers to this as a trade secret, but I see it as confusion, leaving consumers zero chance to make an educated decision. Phthalates leave me dizzy from the questions spinning in my head. If one of the ways we are exposed is through inhalation, and our EPA regulates phthalates as pollutants in air and water, why not regulate them for personal care products? Shouldn't that air quality also encompass the hairspray cloud confined in my small bathroom?

As a mom and consumer, I like to think of phthalates and parabens as the high fructose corn syrup (HFCS) of the beauty aisle. HFCS is an unnecessary ingredient in many foods, but with awareness and effort, I can remove it from my diet, leaving me with simple, healthier-for-me foods. Similarly, parabens and phthalates are unnecessary additives in many body care products and plastics. Starting to remove, replace, or avoid them can guide me along the road to simpler, kinder products. Adding insult to injury (literally), products labeled "unscented" may contain masking ingredients to cover the odor of other chemicals, creating a non-smell. Unless the products proudly announce they are "phthalate free" or use essential oils, the first step in Home Eco-Momics 101 is to choose products labeled "fragrance free." This doesn't solve the problem of course, but it can help you eliminate as many phthalates as possible from your daily use.

By mid-term of my first year exploring household eco-health, I was pleased with my tiny triumphs, as I evaluated and replaced products on my bathroom shelf. With gleeful relief, I still wore deodorant. I still applied makeup, although intentionally less. I occasionally painted my nails various shades of rose, but I often chose to go bare. While I might have been the only one who could notice, for the first time since high school, I stopped wearing foundation. My skin felt happier now that it could breathe, looking healthy on its own merit. With these nuggets of information swimming in my mind, I located the right aisles to shop for lip-stain and shampoo at my local Target. I kept an eye out for sales and clearance stickers, and when I found them, I stocked up.

As I branched out of my bathroom and down the hall, new-to-us brands and differently shaped bottles became permanent residents in our home. This caused some questioning from my family. New textures and scents evoked cries of doubt, "Mom what happened to the old toothpaste?" or "What is this bottle in the shower? Shampoo or body wash?" and even, "This soap smells different." I'd chirp to my family, "Change is good!" Sometimes I would feed them tidbits of what I had learned; that when ingredients from the "old" products were removed, including synthetic preservatives, we might notice changes in product texture. I reassured them there was a reason for all these little changes. Some products like hand soaps and shampoos may be more condensed and require some water and hand rubbing to create lather. Some lotions might feel a bit greasy at first, because they lacked the chemical "penetrators" of many commercial lotions. I found myself educating my family on the myths and assumptions we were programmed to accept as true. Contrary to popular belief (even mine), soaps and cleansers didn't need to foam or lather in order to work effectively. Hair did not have to smell like berries or honeysuckle to be clean. Toothpaste did not have to be blue and gelatinous to eradicate tartar. Selecting simpler was the new household mantra.

My daughter, entranced by Disney teen glamour, asked, "Can I wear nail polish?" Winding my arm around hers and taking this journey together as she becomes a tween will be worthy of its own book. It is a challenge to nurture self-esteem in the high-pressure world of glamour marketing. This will be one more challenge to work through. For now, my simplest response was, "You know how there is junk food and healthy food? Right now, the world is learning there are junk cosmetics and better-for-you cosmetics. When it is time, I'll teach you how to put nail polish on, but I need to find the best brand for you, okay?" Mommy needed some time to learn first.

While change is what I was pursuing, it was a learning curve that sometimes took a little experimenting. Once, excited about free shipping on a bug repellent we hadn't tried before, I ordered a dozen bottles with the intention of applying it from spring baseball to fall soccer. Unfortunately, the putty-colored liquid smelled of minty cat urine. The stench kept away mosquitoes all right, and my entire family as well—the kids ran from me with screams of "Ewww! Gross!" Well, I can't win them all. I decided to stick with my usual brand, knowing it wouldn't leave my children smelling like a litter box.

Sure, it would be nice to have more control over our homes—what we encounter, what enters our bodies. But not at the expense of feeling guilty for not doing enough. Change—whether weight loss, financial stability, or turning a cluttered home into a clean, cozy, happy place—takes time and love for yourself. This applies to working through an eco-health makeover as well. Feeling guilty for not exercising as much as your neighbor, not recycling as passionately as your friend, or not decorating as creatively as your sister, doesn't do you any good. No one seems to know this better than Marla, aka "FlyLady."* Fly is an acronym for Finally Loving

* You can find out more about FlyLady at www.Flylady.net.

Yourself, and hundreds of thousands of her followers (known as FlyBabies) have confronted change under the nurturing of FlyLady's wings. Her philosophy is about establishing little habits that string together into simple routines. FlyLady reassures followers, "Your home did not get cluttered overnight, and it is not going to get clean in a day." It sounds like such a basic concept, and yet many of us don't want to start something unless we know we can do it perfectly and in record speed. I understood I wouldn't be able to overhaul my entire house in a single day, or even a single week, but it didn't stop me from *wanting* to do it that quickly. FlyLady's underlying theme to take care of yourself lovingly weaves in with my quest to celebrate the small wins in any arduous challenge. When we realize that life doesn't have to be such a race and that reaching small milestones makes a big difference, anything is possible.

And so my journey goes. Like anything worthwhile in life, making the changes in my family's bathroom shelves was a process that required a bit of time and patience. Many times, the answers I was looking for just didn't exist yet. The perfect database. The perfect sunscreen. The perfect world. But little changes were good. I did what I could each day. I continued to learn, be wary, and challenge my choices. It continues to be an evolving process, but as long as I'm moving forward, I'm headed in the right direction. There once was a time of uncomplicated products—when families ate simple, unprocessed foods and used straightforward cleaning ingredients—and I like to think there will be a time in the future when we can all choose the wiser way. Our current lives happen to exist in a time of change. We are the sandwiched generation.

My Makeover

Sometimes a dreary, dark grey cloud hovers over my head, like the dirt cloud that surrounds Pig Pen from the Peanuts cartoon, sapping the joy from me and replacing it with crankiness. Once I notice my mood bubble, I often have to dig down to find the cause, and it isn't always obvious. One bleak winter morning, the outdoor weather wasn't giving me much of a lift. Whipping Arctic winds created a wind chill close to zero and kept me housebound. I should have been focusing on the positives. I should have been pleased there were paraben-free shampoos and lotions without fancy-schmancy smells. I should have relished in my lead-free, rhubarb lip tint. I should have been filled with small pride over saving money from using much, much less. Instead, I was grumbling inside and felt emotionally hung-over.

A bleak conversation from the evening before selfishly kidnapped my joy. I had tentatively tried revealing my domestic experiment with women at my son's piano lesson. I extended an invitation for them to join me on my yellow brick road journey, thinking, the more the merrier. They weren't exactly jumping up and down to join me.

"It is really pretty overwhelming. I just wonder if it will really make a difference."

"I believe you, Kristi; it's just not for me. Things are too crazy with the kids right now."

"We are just trying to get by—I can't spend extra money—I mean, we would love to, but we just can't." Then the final statement hit home; "I think we are good, we recycle."

I'm a huge proponent of recycling, but what I was trying to describe to them was a new shade of green. A blurry grey-green, and I evidently wasn't doing a very good job explaining it.

I completely empathized with their responses. Who wanted to tackle the seemingly insurmountable? Instead of allowing enthusiasm to make a mess of my words and thoughts, I needed to think about how to best share what I knew with friends. Eight minutes before the music lesson was over did not make for the right place or time.

These were intelligent, caring, amazing women. I understood it was easier—choosing to remain unacquainted with the facts does make life simpler. Because once we know something, we can't not know it. Which leaves us with two choices: make positive changes to our lifestyle by switching up what we use and purchase, or continue using products with full knowledge of what they contain and could possibly do to our health. Not knowing was effortless. But I truly felt that if my friends really knew what I knew, they'd be willing to join me on this journey. I simply hadn't conveyed my thoughts well enough.

Now feeling very much alone and slouched in my swiveling office chair, I was antsy and fidgety. I obsessively clicked the mouse, tapped my fingers, and wiggled my body. Normally anti-couch potato, here I was a keyboard tator-tot, sitting on my haunches, wasting time. What was my problem? I was ready to do something, anything, to keep moving forward. The only problem was, I still wasn't quite sure what that looked like.

On my computer, the blinking cursor hovered on the website for the Campaign for Safe Cosmetics, taunting me. You know you are losing it when you think inanimate objects like cursors are trying to send you messages. The prefixes for the contact numbers were out of San Francisco, except for one; the Organizing Director had a 617 number— a Boston prefix. Interesting. Just down the road. I was curious, took it as a sign, and dialed the number. A female answered, and my words spilled frenetically. "I made changes. It's going well. I know others would care if they knew. How do I help? Oh, but I am not an expert. I am not a scientist. And I hardly have time to spare." I wrapped up my monologue with an exasperated plea, "I guess I want to do something bigger, I CAN FEEL IT, but I don't know what to do."

There. I said it. More like burped it to a complete stranger. Admittedly, it was not the smoothest of moves and probably sealed my image as a raving lunatic with a bullhorn and soapbox standing in a subway tunnel. I was waiting for the dial tone, but thankfully, it didn't come. On the other end was Mia Davis, the Organizing Director for the Campaign for Safe Cosmetics. She had actually listened. For over an hour, she encouraged and inspired me and fed me morsels of confidence. She explained where I could start and reassured me that I didn't have to be an expert to make an impact. I just had to be a caring human who wanted change.

I pulled myself up, straightened my back, and placed my feet flat on the floor. The dirty, weighty cloud surrounding me dissipated. I felt a jerk—a mental cha-clunk like a roller coaster's chain engaging the gears. The answer had been inside me (it always is). I just needed help defining it. I could now put words to my vision—my goal suddenly became clear.

I wanted to reach out and educate the busy moms, the working women, the Everyday-Me's.

I wanted to inspire women to make little changes, to choose wiser products, and to find their own path within this movement. I decided to start with my community and build to surrounding towns. There would be no doom and gloom messages, no scare tactics; just the facts and ways they could start making changes. Fever and adrenalin building, I loved this vision. This was ME. I brainstormed ideas, filling a notebook with stream-of-conscious thoughts. Thoughts became notes, notes became guidelines, and my philosophy emerged.

I couldn't pretend to be an expert. I was simply an everyday mom and wife who cared about my health, my family's health, and the environment. I would connect the gaps between the experts, the scientists, and the everyday consumer, using the needs of my reluctant friends at piano lessons as a focus. It didn't have to be difficult or expensive. I would prove you didn't have to break the bank for every healthy purchase. Exceptions were out there, but most of the changes I had made in the last few months were not only better for me but also price-comparable to my old products.

With mentoring from the Campaign for Safe Cosmetics, I went to work creating a workshop. Much had changed in the world since I transitioned from Training Manager at Garden Botanika to Director of Household Events. Gone were the days of VHS training tapes. I taught myself PowerPoint by watching my son, Tanner, do homework. This required a screen; yet I didn't have any revenue. I found a 1970s portable projector screen for five dollars on Craigslist. Instead of hotel conference rooms, I used school cafeterias and libraries. Instead of glossy promotional materials, I relied on, well, just faith. I trusted that if I offered the class, someone would come. I was ready. Wasn't that all you needed for an inspirational, educational presentation? Some PowerPoint slides and a forty-year-old screen?

Well, almost. I was ready for that presentation the way a five-year-old is ready for kindergarten—holding a rusty, metal lunchbox containing an apple and some crackers, a newly sharpened pencil, and a box of eight crayons. A new-to-school kindergartener doesn't even know what she doesn't know—isn't really aware of what she needs—but jumps on that bus in the morning with eager anticipation and blind faith. That's how I entered my first presentation on the elementary school library stage in front of eighteen friends. The experience was excruciating for them and for me. Granted, an introduction to toxic chemicals will never warrant a rousing, standing ovation, but my delivery was serious, academic, and depressing. I think back to how I tormented those wonderful people and I'm just grateful they are still friendly to my face. I had asked each person to provide honest feedback. What emotions did they feel? How was my delivery? Did I project? Were my mannerisms natural? What did my body language say? Their honesty made a difference. With their supportive comments, I revamped and revamped and revamped my material.

My challenge was to make academic-sounding toxins an innocuous, commonplace topic of conversation. I dreamed of women meeting for coffee and starting a conversation with, "Amy! So great to see you! How's your quest for sodium laurel sulfate-free shampoo going? Oh, and would your family like to come over for a barbeque Saturday night?"

How could I encourage women to feel safe and comfortable sharing their own insecurities and concerns within their groups of friends? Once we women start talking, we calm insecurities, we share, we learn. How could I introduce toxins and change? Chemicals and inspiration? Somber messages with upbeat me? How could I mesh these opposites into a cohesive presentation?

I pulled out one of the cancer-patient perks: the right to laugh at sacred, inappropriate times. Mock seriousness until the subject was commonplace or crack jokes about chemo's super powers. A sarcastic, humorous approach left my husband and me giggling through cancer treatments as we took liberty with endless double entendres regarding ta-tas, racks, and headlights. With all this body part rebuilding, I was like the Bionic Woman. Or, one of these chemo infusions must have a strength-enhancing side effect, like repelling all future mosquitoes from wanting a taste of my blood! I needed to infuse humor into my presentation. Humor, along with stories and a visual prop of homemade toxic stew (a glass jar, dog food, and water), turned the message upside down—turned it into me, presenting a "do-what-you-can-do" platform.

Within three months, I hit the roads of my community with my Choose Wiser workshop. My presentation was cheesy, maybe even hokey, but it was what I had. Women bravely invited me into their circle of friends: the Mom's Club, a book club, and a house party over appetizers and wine. Ladies attended on the encouragement of the host or simply as an excuse for an evening out. Fine by me. I relished the energy that pulsed through their chatter and questions. I knew I had uncovered something special and important.

I refined my presentations by joining a local chapter of Toastmasters to develop my public speaking skills. I replaced my kindergarten lunch carrier with a tricked-out Bento box full of colorful produce. I traded in my set of eight crayons for the box containing 144 with a built-in sharpener. Soon, the curious started inviting me: the local karate school, the Women's Business Network, and nurses at my own Faulkner Hospital. My workshops continued to share facts and reports through stories. What made them inspiring was the message—to choose wiser, select simpler, and respect the body. Those truths resonate within all of us, whether or not we are ready to accept them.

I believe in the Everyday-Me's. I believe people really want to live a more healthful life and provide that for their children. I just want to wake up what already exists and try to reassure others that it doesn't have to be a painful, difficult, expensive proposition. With every workshop and every testimonial, I hold on tightly, knowing the California girl in me is surfing the thin edge of a very powerful wave.

Devour

But imagine for a moment if we once again knew, strictly as a matter of course, these few unremarkable things: What it is we're eating. Where it came from. How it found its way to our table. And what, in a true accounting, it really cost.

~Michael Pollan, The Omnivore's Dilemma

The Ride Down

Taxol receded in my mind's rearview mirror, chasing after the chemotherapy that started nearly a year ago. The decrease in medication gave my body room to breathe, stretch, and heal. I found myself slowly growing out of re-birth and heading toward a teenage growth spurt, complete with continued hair growth and sleep cravings. I relived junior high excitement, watching leg hair resume its rightful place after being blasted from its follicles. As I ran my fingertips up my tibia, I thought, *How I adore these little whiskers!* My razor, old and gross from a summer without use, stayed in the medicine cabinet, as I opted for au natural armpit tufts and scratchy legs. The hairier, granola version of me lasted less than a week before I was darting out of the shower to rummage for my husband's razor, leaving puddles on the tile floor. I traded new-hair-growth appreciation for finally-shaving-again excitement; I gingerly went to work toward nick-free ankles and sleek calves.

And I slept. Oh, how I slept! In the mornings, I'd scrunch under my comforter and slumber for twenty more minutes as my children skittered to the clank of cereal bowls. After lunch, I sought out sunshine streaming through windows onto my Berber carpet and curled into the angular warmth for a nap. If I were a cat, I would have flicked the tip of my tail in bliss. Autumn's nightfall descended earlier now, and I was seduced into the bedroom craving slumber's intoxication. After the crap I had been through, it was perfectly allowable. Utterly justifiable. I gave myself permission to sleep the month away.

My husband would fervently agree I am a passionate woman by nature—one who peaks in the exhilarating highs of go-go-go and then craves isolation and solitude. Quite possibly within the span of a single weekend. However, as Halloween came and went, my pendulum seemed to be stuck. My excessive sleep morphed into a constant fog and muddled my ambition. Laundry piled. The refrigerator politely begged to be refilled with each opening of the door.

Posing the kids for Christmas cards would entail way too much work this year. Even my binder-paper list lay abandoned in my right hand drawer. When I should have been pondering what I was thankful for this year—and I had a bounty worth—I was void, empty. My typically social-self declined invitations to cookie swaps and Christmas parties. An invisible girdle constricted my lungs making it difficult to breathe. As soon as school bus fumes dissipated after morning drop-off, tears flowed as if on cue. The ache started in my bone marrow, and tears surfaced at the ducts. Then they streamed, silently. No emotion. No sobbing. No drama. Something was happening to me, yet the disturbing part was I didn't care. I was the oblivious frog in a pot with moist, bulbous eyes staring blankly as tepid temperatures dangerously increased.

One particularly weepy day, it was too much to put my daughter on the bus. Really, it didn't require much—a fifth of a mile, a three-point turn, and return—but where would I find that kind of energy? My inner-me was infinitesimal now—buried beneath the heaviness of sleep, tears, and emptiness. With a tiny voice, she pleaded not to let the fog affect my children. *I need help!* she cried. She reached out of the suffocating sludge for a hand up; I finally told my husband what had been happening in my head.

My family grabbed my wrist, pulled me to solid ground, and concluded, "Depression! Of course. Finally pushing through repressed emotions." Doctors reassured, "This is normal. What you went through was traumatic. This can happen years out." The psychiatrist scribbled prescriptions for anti-depressants instructing, "Try this, then we can adjust the dosages over the next few months."

Maybe there was truth to their theories. After all, they had an outside perspective I lacked. A wiser voice in my head intervened before I popped pills. Two-thirds down my trusty to-do list, I made a ground-kissing discovery. Autumn had coincided with the start of my monthly Leuprolide shot meant to keep cancer recurrence at bay by reducing my estrogen production. I had opted for the shot versus an oophorectomy, thinking the shot would be less hassle for my family and one less surgery for me. It seemed harmless, innocent even, just one day a month to drop my drawers for a tiny burn in my right buttock. Yet, this stealthy little drug slyly hijacked my persona and wove a dark, synthetic depression out of my hormones.

I skipped the next shot, testing my theory that this was the cause of my depression. The real me ripped darkness into shreds with hulk-ish strength. I was exuberant. Passionate. After four months of descent, I loved my life again. My pendulum swung full force into long-lasting giddiness. It felt so good to be me! I never want to endure that suffocation again, and I would not wish it on anyone. Without the discovery of this coincidence, I would have continued to experiment with a range of anti-depressants, masking the real cause.

With deep irony, there it was. I had become the perfect laboratory of all I studied. Parts per billion. Accumulation. Unknown side effects. Manipulation of hormones. I chuckled. *Okay, Life. Two points to your side. I bow to your shrewdness, your twisted humor. But why use me as a human Petri dish? Pretty dangerous, don't ya think?*

In terms of keeping my body cancer-free, an oophorectomy was now my only option. This surgery would remove my ovaries and starve potential cancer cells by reducing estrogen production. It would also be my seventh surgery, and I had to admit, I was taking a liking to the euphoria of anesthesia. There weren't many enjoyable phases of surgery, but anesthesia was one of them. I smiled at the thought of watching the bright, stainless steel lights from the gurney and the metal taste in my mouth. I knew I would barely hear the nurse lean over me to ask, "Are you doing all right honey?" as powerful drugs pulled me into sleep.

Before I eagerly held out my wrist for the hospital admittance bracelet, I scrupulously reviewed the long-term effects of living sans ovaries. In short, it would consist of a car-crash style menopause. This process normally took years but would now be compressed into a few months. I prepared for whatever tailspin side effects my body wanted to drag me through—tossing and turning, drenching night sweats, wringing out my clothes. Interrupting conversations to declare how hot it was, fanning my flushed face, losing concentration on the topic. Playing thermostat tag with my husband. Pushing through physical side effects would just take time.

Mentally, I had to contemplate what it meant to have my beloved ovaries plucked. I hadn't given much thought to my olive-sized reproductive parts before, but suddenly they were my dearest body part. I had already lost my breast tissue, my hair, a dozen lymph nodes, and thousands of cells (which for some reason hadn't added up to any weight loss), and now I had to figure out how to live without my olives. What would this mean for my future?

These mystical ovaries harbored possible descendants. Who were the millions of potential-baby-eggs nestled deep inside? How many of them had Tanner's peace and humor? Kyle's joy and twinkle? Were there eggs with Kate's confidence and strength? Admittedly, I was a better mother to those who slept through the night than those who had yet to learn. From deep inside, far beyond my reproductive system, I found acceptance. No more babies would ripen within my uterus. I'd trade the option of newborns for the chance to raise my three current children. It was an easy sacrifice.

With my oophorectomy behind me, I prepared for the hormonal crashing I'd read about. *Wait for it*, I warned. *Hormonal whiplash may take a few days, or even a couple of weeks.* I proceeded with caution over the next month, but it never came. With the tying of neat little sutures, menopause was over before it even started. Maybe Mother Life felt apologetic over the mock depression. Maybe this was the frosting on my Devil's Chocolate Cancer cake. Menopause was one life experience I would have to live without.

The drug-induced depression was pivotal. Not for what it taught me but for what it allowed me to do. During those winter months, incarcerated in my home and shackled by depression, my temporary persona pulsed one thought: escape. I melted into Michael Pollan's *Omnivore's Dilemma,* a four hundred-page odyssey. Like a bug perched on his shoulder, I hungrily turned pages and traveled through farms, feedlots, pastures, and woodlands, seeing them as a naturalist and enraptured by Pollan's storytelling. The dilemma of being an omnivore—having choices in food sources—planted a seed within me. Had I been so consumed by what I lathered, smeared, and wiped onto my body that I didn't pay attention to what I spooned into my mouth? Nutrition wise, I thought I was a B+ student, doing pretty well. Purging my cupboards certainly couldn't be as complicated as deciphering Lola Lolita Pink nail polish. After all, hadn't we been asking, "What's for dinner?" for thousands of years? Breathless, I continued reading, as Pollan's message echoed my own shopping-induced anxiety.

> Somehow this most elemental of activities—figuring out what to eat—has come to require a remarkable amount of expert help. How did we ever get to a point where we need investigative journalists to tell us where our food comes from and nutritionists to determine the dinner menu?[44]

Of course feeding a family was complicated. It came with the job description. Was he implying it should or could be simpler? Growing up, I trusted the guidance of food fads, assuming that if it was popular enough to warrant press, it must be advancement in our human evolution. Food philosophies landmarked my life like notches on a kid's growth chart. As a teen, I emulated advice from beauty magazines and avoided fatty eggs, mayonnaise, cheeses, and ranch dressing. During college years, I observed calorie-counting rituals. I filled journals with scribbled shorthand notations: "80 cal. morning mocha. 70 cal. yogurt." I always abandoned the tedious record keeping after a week. As a new mother, I fancied "Super Foods" and devoured books with succulent, full-color pictures of miracle-producing foods like avacados, almonds, and blueberries. I was lured by thoughts that if I ate enough of these foods, my nursing children would develop into valedictorians and live to be one hundred and two. Eventually, I left this philosophy behind too, and then forged into product label reading.

By the time I could buckle my oldest son, Tanner, into the shopping cart, I should have earned an honorary degree in label scanning for deciphering the sides of food packages. My eyes darted between sodium, saturated fat, and fiber content before selecting a box of flakes, krispies, or o's. While running errands one day with my mother, she commented on my behavior. She thought reading labels was peculiar, not to mention time consuming. Until she voiced her observation, I hadn't realized that past generations didn't have to read labels to understand their food. Contemporary nutritional labels became part of food packaging in just 1993, and a new mothering skill was born. How did my mother and her mother know what they were dishing up? I realized I had deciphered labels because our family was eating food that required deciphering. Lucky me.

Where had all these fads gotten me? Did cutting out eggs in my diet when I was a teen help me to have slender adult thighs today? Did those Super Foods make it through my breast milk and into my children, enabling them to respond with witty retorts to my requests? Was reading food labels a skill I could be proud to talk about at dinner parties over martinis and mini meatballs on toothpicks? Well, yes and no. The label reading was an effective tool for me when trying to figure out how to reduce sodium, even if it made my shopping trips a bit longer. I realized the time I invested comparing fish vs. animal shaped crackers masked the bigger observation. When should we step back and challenge, *Is this really food at all?* If an edible product is on the grocery store shelves, it must be food, right?

While the bathroom closet overhaul I initiated felt overwhelming at times, I was titillated about a fresh mental expedition. I loved food! Yet part of me was reluctant to jump in too eagerly. I had easily reduced the amount of cosmetics I used, but giving up food could be counterproductive to my health. Karen made my skin care products;

would she would raise a cow for me as well? In terms of convenience, I had a grocery store within a stone's throw of my house. Would I now have to drive fifty minutes to get to the closest natural health store for tofu and sprouts? Bottom line was, I prided myself on being an all-American coupon-clipping-penny-pincher. My own skepticism of hoity-toity organic food and its swollen prices forecasted this might be a quick trip down the aisle and back over to budget-central. Besides, didn't we need to use chemicals in mass food production to feed our rapidly augmenting population? What miserable lunch packing battles lay ahead if I changed my family's food? Yet, I was tempted by the glimmer-of-hope that family dinnertime could become simpler, easier, or more joyful.

I pumped up my psyche and chanted lessons I'd learned from the lavatory purge. *It is a journey, not a to-do list. I am safer today than I was yesterday. Find what works, transfer it to the grocery list, and move on. And remember: pat yourself on the back and say good job.* Still, despite my desire to continue moving our family toward a more nontoxic lifestyle, the little girl within me tugged at my sweater asking, *"But why? Why do I have to study? Why do I have to learn what to eat? It's not supposed to be this difficult to feed and raise a family, is it?"*

A Sprinkle of This

As a kid, it was a family competition to be the first person to spy a small airplane swooping acrobatically across farmlands on a road trip. Even though we were safe within our station wagon, we would duck our heads as the pilot brazenly crossed over the highway to dust crops with chemicals and powder my future lunches. These particles went to work repelling evil bugs, suffocating relentless weeds, or supercharging plant growth. While every juicy strawberry, prickly artichoke, or bunch of grapes in my Brady Bunch lunchbox was a result of chemical farming, it was new to the twentieth century. After World War II, we innovatively repurposed weapons designed for battle into food chain supplements. Pollan had educated, "The government encouraged conversion of the munitions industry to fertilizer—ammonium nitrate being the main ingredient of both bombs and chemical fertilizer—and the conversion of nerve-gas research to pesticides."[45] Insecticides, herbicides, and fungicides were used abundantly in the following decades—appropriately earning the nickname of "Pesticide Era"—and revolutionized not just agriculture but just about every aspect of our contemporary food chain.

By the time I could drive through a Taco Bell on my own, pesticide usage had increased fifty-fold. The Environmental Protection Agency website explained succinctly, "By their very nature, most pesticides create some risk of harm. Pesticides can cause harm to humans, animals, or the environment because they are designed to kill or otherwise adversely affect living organisms."[46] Today over one billion tons of pesticide products made from nine hundred active ingredients, many of which are toxic,[47] are used annually in the United States.[48] It's not difficult to understand how the Beyond Pesticide website elaborates and connects an industry with its origins in nerve gas and poisons to the increase in Alzheimer's, asthma, birth defects, cancer, diabetes, learning and developmental issues, Parkinson's, and reproductive health problems.[49]

What to do? What to do? How should I approach this massive subject? I could focus on health effects from wordy reports. A study at Harvard University found an increased risk for attention deficit hyperactivity disorder (ADHD) in children exposed to typical levels of organophosphates—the main component in insecticides.[50] Or, perhaps I could spend my time sifting through individual pesticides. Atrazine, for example, a popular herbicide, is an endocrine disruptor.[51] The United States uses an estimated seventy-five million pounds of it each year, even though the European Union banned its usage in 2005. How was I supposed to understand which pesticide had been used on which veggie at the grocery store? Did I even want to know?

Attracted to simpler guidelines, I started with the Environmental Working Group (EWG) and its ability to regurgitate scientific findings into wallet cards and catchy top ten lists. EWG kindly offered to break down pesticide residues into juicy, easy-to-swallow bites. My first lesson was to learn that washing and peeling fruits and vegetables wasn't always effective. Many pesticides were absorbed by the plant and resided inside. Of course, I still washed these foods before we ate them but not for the removal of pesticides exclusively.

The second thing I learned was that certain fruits and vegetables might contain more pesticides than others. EWG tested fifty-three fruits and vegetables and ranked them by their likelihood of being consistently contaminated with the greatest number of pesticides. The results were labeled the "Dirty Dozen" and included such snacking pleasures as celery, peaches, and strawberries. The opposite of the Dirty Dozen was the "Clean Fifteen"—those fruits and vegetables found with the lowest amount of residual contamination—including onions, avocados, and sweet corn. Easy to download and share, these lists quickly became popular reference materials and media fodder.

There was a small, media backlash over the Dirty Dozen list, suggesting consumers would purge their homes of fruits and vegetables like lead paint. I brushed this off and wished the media would give us consumers a little more credit. Never had I heard, "Put that apple down, Johnny! We don't eat fruits; they are full of chemicals." I thought I would find alternatives to the Dirty Dozen and shop contentedly for the Clean Fifteen, but even that dismisses the EWG's big picture. "Pesticides are toxic by design. They are created expressly to kill living organisms—insects, plants, and fungi considered 'pests.' Many pesticides pose health dangers to people."[52] Choosing the cantaloupe, sweet peas, or other produce *lightly* sprinkled with synthetic chemicals, brushes aside chemical farming's unintended environmental atrocities.

Chemicals not absorbed by the plant can move upward into wildlife. Similar to our Western Grebe story, Carbofuran alone (an extremely toxic pesticide used on corn and potatoes) is reported to be involved in the deaths of more than forty species of birds, including robins, larks, sparrows, cardinals, goldfinches, bluebirds, blackbirds, and doves. Secondary poisoning—poisoning resulting from ingestion of poisoned insects and small birds—has been reported in owls, hawks, and eagles.[53] In the 1980s, the EPA estimated that the pesticide was killing between one and two million birds per year.*[54] The EPA finally banned Carbofuran for food crops in the United States at the end of 2009, but it is not the lone offender.

It doesn't stop there. Our toxin trail descends into our waterways, moving from streams to rivers to oceans. Here, the runoff from chemical farming depletes water of oxygen until it cannot support marine life.[55] Runoff from the Mississippi River into the Gulf of Mexico alone has created a seven thousand square mile seasonal wildlife "Dead Zone." Sadly, Dead Zones are now dotting our planet's coastlines and have been doubling every ten years since the 1960s,[56] contributed to by the Dirty Dozen, the Clean Fifteen, and everything in between.

It was disheartening to reflect on what we were doing, but I will uncomfortably admit that it wasn't enough to change my ingrained ways. I needed options, open doors to provide direction. Unfortunately, living off the land was not an option for my family. If we had to rely on my ability to grow things, my family would wither away. I, undeniably, have a black thumb. I'm sure lettuce in my fridge wilts faster simply because it is under my care. I don't even own a household fern or philodendron—the plants that thrive in the worst of conditions and are (apparently) impossible to kill. If it's green and relies on photosynthesis for survival, it's sure to meet its demise upon crossing into my own domestic Dead Zone. I harbor jealousy of my friends who have options

---

* "In the 1980s the EPA estimated that the pesticide was killing up to 1 million or 2 million birds a year, and the Fish and Wildlife Service reported that there was no safe way to use the chemical without killing migratory birds. In 1991 the EPA moved to ban the most widely used method of application of the chemical, grains spread over the ground, which birds ingested. But the ban was pushed back to 1996, and some exemptions were granted through 2006. When the EPA moved to cancel the pesticide's registration in 2006, which would end all uses in the United States, its manufacturer, FMC Corporation, and allies in Congress opposed the decision in court and lobbied for help from the Bush Administration in 2008."

as they effortlessly grow herbs on their patio, tend vertical gardens in the city, or nurture snacking gardens in their backyards. I was starting to think I had to chalk this area up to "just the way it is" or "not much I can do."

To Be or Not To Be

One evening, in between the clinking of dinner dishes and mild sibling taunting, my daughter asked, "Mom, are you organic?" Here she was asking me, a self-professed educator on toxin-free living, for wisdom. I paused for thought. Her question was elementary, but my answer was complex. I was stuck, mumbling, "Uh, um…uh…" My lack of maternal wisdom in this embarrassing moment challenged me to reflect on the seemingly simple question, "Mom, are you organic?"

Was I?

For most of my life, my interpretation of the term *organic* was not a practice or a movement, but a label. A loose, slang description interchangeable with granola, crunchy, vegan, or tree-hugger. Maybe woo-woo, out-there, flowy flower girl. It stemmed from my youth, living within driving distance of proud-hippie towns like Santa Cruz and Berkeley, California. Towns dotted with open-air restaurants serving homemade multigrain bread with avocado and kale juice smoothies. The patrons were a mixed assortment of dreadlocks, surfboards, and earthy body odor. In our Northern California culture, I had inferred, depending on the voice inflection, that being organic could be a compliment or a condemnation.

This definition broadened as an adult student at the Rhode Island School of Design. My classmates loosely used the term *organic* during group critiques. The safe, yet ambiguous response when called on was a dramatic pause for reflection partnered with, "I love the organic quality to the lines." The word wasn't about dreadlocks or bean sprouts anymore but referenced a feeling that came from the fluidity and flow of our oil paintings. While it was difficult to describe exactly what made a painting organic, it seemed to be an academic response when you had no other answer at hand.

I was pretty sure my daughter wasn't asking if I had ever owned a VW bus or smelled like an onion in summer. While she's a good artist, I didn't think she was seeking artistic advice on how to color a picture that defied convention. I could go with, "We are all organic matter my love, living organisms, capable of growth and decay," but that sounded a little philosophical, even if it was technically true. When it came right down to it, I was not organic in the sense she was asking. Okay. I'll say it aloud. I did not purchase organic food. I had little knowledge of how my food was grown. In my conventional produce section, they didn't advertise whether or not the fresh crop of strawberries was "Atrazine sprinkled." Signs usually indicated where the food came from, but I wasn't empowered with the knowledge of individual countries' farming standards. At least items labeled "USDA Certified Organic" had legal definitions, while the words *natural* or *natural ingredients* had no legal definition and could mean many different things from product to product. I was conventionally clueless about how my mainstream produce was grown.

At the time, my association to the word *organic* meant high prices and the derogatory phrase "food snob." The closest I steered my shopping cart to that lonely organic island in the middle of my opulent produce section, was to push right on by and espouse how ridiculous the prices were. "$6.99 a pound for organic cherries! That's crazy!" I'd continue my voyage to the seventy-five foot row of misted, conventional produce to save a buck. It was habit. All the while my mind warned, *You can't compare an organic apple to a traditional apple; they are no longer the same. Remember the pesticides? Remember the Dead Zones? Think about what you add to your plate when you are trying to save a dime!*

The mental battle between what was good for my body and what was good for my short-term budget was enough to give me a headache. Maybe a more mindful, aware shopper would have opened her pocketbook and heart after learning of birds dying. But I balked. I wavered. Until I finally hit bottom with a little elementary education in GMOs—an acronym I was sure didn't have anything to do with MY grocery list. Or I guess you could say, when I discovered the OMG in GMOs.

Waiter, There's a GMO In My Soup!

Here and there, my eyes would run across the acronym GMO, barely acknowledge it, and move right past the letters. I wasn't sure what it meant or entailed—other than something had been genetically modified. I employed every justification technique to avoid tackling the subject:

- Any term with the word *genetic* in it was way above my head.
- I would read about it next week.
- GMOs must exist for some reason (like astronaut food), but surely it wasn't in my food.
- I had labels down pat, and my food didn't refer to any Recommended Daily Values of GMOs.

Avoidance of the subject didn't make the enigma disappear. Like testing the temperature of a lake with my toes, I cautiously broached the conversation among intelligent, respected confidants. Surely, they would educate me in the intimacy of our own private conversation without mocking my knowledge of current events. Then I wouldn't feel quite so ignorant. Refilling glasses of wine, I tentatively asked, "So. What do you know about GMOs?" Unsure themselves and wondering why we weren't discussing the Red Sox, they shrugged their shoulders.

I pushed back gently to encourage my version of stimulating conversation: "From what I understand, a plant's DNA can be altered to resist weed killers. Then, the farmer who sows the altered seeds can spray the crop with weed killers, and the plant comes through just dandy." I paused to let my polite audience catch up on my play-by-play. "I just want to know, am I supposed to be concerned about eating altered plants?"

My dearest friend soaked up my roundabout statement and replied, "I guess I would be concerned if I found out my food was sprayed with pesticides."

Thunk.

That wasn't the answer I was expecting. I was caught off guard. All the lessons I had recently learned flashed through my head and raced toward my mouth in what could have been a passionate soapbox dissertation.

"Yes," I replied slowly, and then reflectively added, "Yes, I too would be concerned about pesticides."

I hoped I wasn't condescending. In that brief conversation there was a lot I needed to absorb. First, I wasn't the only one who was unfamiliar with GMOs. I found comfort in our equal ignorance. Or so I thought. The bigger revelation was realizing that many of us know so little about our own food sources. Evidently, as a newly-appointed advocate for my own human body (and maker of the family meals), it was up to me to self-educate and find out why this subject was so alien. I enrolled in a training course offered by international author and GMO expert, Jeffrey Smith, from the Institute for Responsible Technology. My goal was to learn about and demystify the elusive acronym. Then, regurgitate the ABCs of GMOs to others.

From my scribbled notes, I broke down the basics of GMOs:

- ❖ GMO is the acronym for a genetically modified organism, also referred to as genetic engineering (GE) or genetic modification (GM). What a relief! I only had to decipher one acronym, not three.
- ❖ GMOs are created when genes from DNA are taken from one species and inserted into the DNA of another species. The DNA's highly specific mission can perform in the new host.
- ❖ Extracted genes may have come from bacteria, viruses, insects, animals, or even humans.

The science and usage of genetic engineering was mind-blowing. We have taken genes from spiders and inserted them into goat DNA in hopes that the goat milk would contain spider web protein for use in bulletproof vests. In another instance, cow genes crossed with pigs turned pigskins into cowhides. Or maybe you heard of the jellyfish genes that lit up pigs' noses in the dark? I've yet to figure out why this would be helpful—except it would be a cool trick during evening barbeques. When it came to food, Arctic fish genes gave tomatoes and strawberries tolerance to frost. (A straw-brrr-y.) Human genes have been inserted into dairy cows to produce milk with human breast milk properties.

We are brilliant humans! Who knew? In fact, I can think of at least a hundred animal qualities that would come in handy in my life. I'd love to inject myself with hummingbird DNA and be able to complete all my daily chores and duties at the speed of lightning. Or slip some bat DNA into my husband, so he'll have finely-tuned listening skills capable of honing in on even my non-verbal female messages. Who wouldn't want to inject their children with a few fish genes, so they would be born natural swimmers, eliminating the potential for drowning forevermore? The possibilities here were endless!

My brain was electrified, crackling with questions. What about my brother's Bernese mountain dog? Was she a GMO? Surely, this was how the Jackalope manifested itself. Could we create a canta-guava-limon? What about those unfamiliar fruits that caught my eye at the grocery store? Did mixing my DNA with my husband's after one romantic getaway produce offspring in this category? Jeffrey Smith clarified that genetic engineering was completely different from traditional breeding and just as importantly, carried unique risks. In traditional breeding, it is possible to mate a pig with another pig to get a new species, but it is not possible to mate a pig with a potato or a mouse. (But don't tell our guinea pig he can't mate with the shoes on the floor. It's his favorite pastime.) When two similar species do breed—a horse and a donkey for example—the offspring, a mule in this case, is usually infertile. Genetic engineering, on the other hand, allows scientists to breach species barriers set by nature. The results are plants or animals with traits that would be virtually impossible to obtain with natural processes such as crossbreeding or grafting.

Fascinatingly complicated, I thought. Maybe this would be a subject I accepted but never mastered, like my mother and her relationship with the DVR remote. As long as you have people around who understand, you can get by. As a modern world topic, maybe my children would carry that gene of understanding. Maybe I could schedule a Girl Scout field trip to one of these immaculate laboratories and watch the precise goings-on of scientists and geneticists behind plate glass windows. As I continued my studies, I was thrown a curveball. I didn't need to visit a laboratory to find examples of genetically modified items. I simply needed to go to any local grocery store. Or, downstairs to my kitchen cabinet, as GMOs were introduced into our food supply in the mid-1990s. As of May 2010, IRT's website shared that current, commercialized GMO crops in the United States included:

- Soy (91%)
- Cotton (71%)
- Canola (88%)
- Corn (85%)
- Sugar beets (90%)
- Hawaiian papaya (more than 50%)
- Alfalfa (currently at Supreme Court)
- Zucchini and yellow squash (small amount)
- Tobacco (Quest® brand)
- Possibly in the near future, salmon

What does that mean for our dinner plates? *Slate* magazine stated, "No government body keeps precise statistics, but a popular guesstimate among university researchers is that around seventy percent of processed foods contain GMO ingredients."[57]

This wasn't going over so well with me. I was all for advancement, until I learned it was crossing over that one-acre property line of mine without being invited. My hands, now highly skilled at product-flipping, went to work as my laser eyes rapidly scanned the front, back, and undersides of boxes, cans, and bottles in my cabinets. Nothing. Not a peep to indicate some or any of the ingredients within might be genetically modified. I was stupefied. You're telling me I can find out if my groceries were made in a nut-free facility or when a beer was born but not if food was made with GMO ingredients? Why weren't these companies proudly stating that my mac n' cheese was enhanced at the hand of a scientist? Where was the former celebrity GMO spokesperson touting health benefits? The picture of the family laboratory proudly producing genetically modified food for a half a generation? The absence of a GMO label led me to believe they weren't in the products I used. If I have the inalienable right to life, and I equate that with the right to health, then I have a right to know. Let's just call this strike one.

While scientists tinker and toil and research behind laboratory walls in controlled settings, cross-contamination occurs every day in the fields, altering neighboring crops. For me, this was strike two. In our biosphere, pollen floats, wind carries, bees share, and birds poop. Pollen from most GMO crops can contaminate nearby organic crops of the same type. We cannot reverse the contamination that has already happened. Due to cross-contamination, there was a very real chance that my right, my choice to decide, would disappear forever. I was nervous my kids would grow up and simply not have the choice to eat non-GMO food if they desired.

What made me uneasy about the GMO food story was it didn't start with the advent of World War II or with my parents' generation. This experimentation with the food chain was on my generation's shoulders, yet few people I knew were informed. Decisions being made by government, corporations, and scientists were happening right now.

Some believe that GMOs could lead to the creation of new toxins or allergens or to changes in nutritional value or pose unforeseen threats to surrounding animals and wildlife. Some crops are engineered to be resistant to herbicides and pesticides, allowing crops to flourish while simultaneously eradicating weeds. Other plants are engineered to produce their own pesticide to kill or deter insects. Some people feel the toxins produced by these crops are far stronger than any found in nature. George Kimbrell, an attorney at the Center for Food Safety, had this to say about GMOs: "They don't help us feed the world, they don't fight climate change, they don't help us better the environment. They just increase [the use of] pesticides and herbicides. That's what they do." [58]

I reflected how our reckless and abundant use of pesticides had influenced oceans, animals, and humans. We were just one decade into deluging our food supply with GMO-based foods. What would happen if we decided in twenty years that genetically modifying our crops and seeds was a terribly wrong decision? Where would we be then? What would our era be referred to, "The GMO Years?" The bottom line for me: GMO foods have not been in use long enough for me to feel convinced they are safe. There are still too many questions surrounding these foods and not nearly enough answers. I felt like I was being asked to play ball with a blindfold on. The unknown was strike three.

The benefit of identifying these issues here and now is that we can make a difference. What Rachel Carson attempted to do with pesticides, Jeffrey Smith is trying to do with GMOs. He believes that although GMOs are one of the most dangerous health and environmental risks we face, they are also one of the easiest to solve. According to Smith, just a small percentage of the population switching to non-GMO brands could create a tipping point, forcing major food companies to quickly replace GMO ingredients. When the tipping point of consumer rejection was reached in Europe in 1999, it became a marketing liability, and within a single week, virtually all-major food companies committed to removing GMOs from their products. While the controversy and data goes far beyond my introductory paragraphs, I passionately want the Everyday-Me's to be aware. With a little GMO knowledge, you can have your own discussions and make your own decisions.

Personally, I am fascinated by science and applaud many advancements. My Herceptin medicine, for example, was approved the same year as my diagnosis, which likely saved my life. But before it dripped into my veins, I understood and accepted all the possible repercussions. Herceptin only interacted with me through my hanging IV drip bag, but GMOs interact with entire food systems without my knowing and understanding the implications and possible outcomes. It's all about *choice*. I should be able to choose whether or not I eat and purchase genetically modified foods; I don't want the decision made for me.

It was now my turn to bat, but without the blinders. Until our government mandates that all food products containing genetically modified ingredients be labeled, my simplest out-of-the-park swing was to buy organic—which does not allow GMO ingredients. Some may claim that the benefits of genetically modified food outweigh the negatives, but the long-term effects of those negatives make me hesitate. While having the speed of a hummingbird seems helpful to me, perhaps it would leave me unable to relax. My husband might listen more attentively to me with his bat-like hearing but would probably sleep all day and be awake at night. And the kids? Well, it's hard enough to get the kids out of the pool now, never mind if they were natural-born swimmers. It might be inconvenient at times, but I'll take my family, and my food, in their most genuine form. After finding out more about GMOs, I was happy to grab a flag and join the non-GMO movement.

Labor To Love

In addition to all this information about GMOs, I came across an encouraging study that helped give me direction. The study found that children who ate an organic diet for just five days, reduced their circulating pesticide endocrine disruptors to undetectable levels.[59] For me, that study sealed the deal—I was going organic. Now I needed one thing: to make this as easy as possible. The freshest organic foods were going to be the ones grown closest to me, and close meant more economical, as I wouldn't be paying for the shipping costs. In the land of California with its temperate weather, there may be plenty of variety within fifty miles, but here in the land of blizzards and humidity, the "local" boundaries were a little farther. I began by searching LocalHarvest.org for options close to my town. I talked with farmers in my area and found I could purchase products grown under conditions that met organic growing standards but weren't necessarily certified organic due to the time or money required to attain certification. It all boiled down to knowing where my fruits and veggies came from and how they were grown. My brother had shared his positive experience with community supported agriculture, more commonly referred to as a CSA, and I decided to start my adventure by following in his footsteps.

Members of a CSA own a share of the crops the farm grows and harvests. By purchasing a share early in the year, the money collected upfront creates a resource for the farmer, allowing him or her to invest in seeds and equipment. In return, each CSA member takes home weekly batches of freshly harvested fruits and vegetables throughout the growing season. Services and items included in a CSA vary from one farm to the next. Some memberships include herbs, flower gardens, honey, orchard fruit, pick your own berries, pumpkin patches, hayrides, eggs, or homemade bread. The downside to a CSA is the shared risk. If unseasonal weather takes down a berry or legume crop, all CSA members are affected, yet if there is a bounty of tomatoes or beans, everyone reaps the reward.

The first year my brother and his family joined, they followed through with meticulous comparisons that I wish I had the patience to initiate. Each week they noted the quantities of spinach, bok choy, cilantro, scallions, or whatever was included in the distribution and then compared those prices to the same food at the grocery store. At the end of the season, the totals were close, but the CSA was slightly cheaper. What was rousing was that the comparison was between the local CSA organic food and conventionally grown produce. I think he was just looking to see the difference in cost, not expecting to find the organic food to be lower in price at the end of the season. There were, of course, many variables in his home experiment, such as the abundance of the shares, the length of Mother Nature's rainy season, or the way his CSA decided on distribution. And granted, it only covered one year. Nevertheless, this was a personal quest from an MIT graduate whom I know to be analytical, impartial, and without motivation to slant the study. Now with more incentive than ever, it was time to sign up for our own CSA share.

Once I purchased a share, each Tuesday from late May to early November our family would head down to the farm to pick up the weekly offering. In many CSA formats, members take what is placed in their shares, versus a farm stand where you can select and purchase what you want. When the season was at its peak, our share easily required one full-size cooler and a couple reusable shopping bags to carry home the treasures. After picking up our first few shares, we learned that locally grown produce is vastly different from the food we were used to bringing home from the grocery store. Items didn't look the same. They didn't smell the same. Honestly, they were a lot more exciting. The limited varieties of produce grown for large-scale markets are bred for uniform shapes, color, and the ability to handle long distance shipping, limiting the consumer experience. Most people don't know that Mother Nature creates tomatoes in colors from green to black or that red and yellow carrots are even more delicious than orange ones. Lettuce isn't always green. Raspberries can be yellow.

Alida Cantor of Langwater Farm, just down the road from my house, explained how biodiversity in our food sources has been lost in our move toward an industrialized food system.

"One of the most important things that was lost was flavor. Nothing compares to the taste of a freshly picked garden tomato. The ones available in the grocery store have been bred to hold their shape and resist bruising during cross-country trips, not because they taste good. Heirloom tomatoes garner the most attention, but there are heirloom varieties of just about every plant, from peppers to squash to turnips to corn. Heirloom varieties often have a specific, attractive quality that led generations of gardeners to save them: they are great for canning or pickling; they are cold hardy and withstand a light frost, or they have excellent flavor. The torpedo-shaped Speckled Roman tomato, for example, is great for sauces, while the giant Striped Germans are best to slice and eat fresh."

In the heat of a summer afternoon, my kids, who don't love tomatoes at home, would line up along the climbing vines of cherry tomatoes to tickle the orbs and watch them fall into the quart container.

We'd move down the rows, picking vibrant red-orange tomatoes, surrounded by the deep herbal fragrance of the plants. Heavy and swollen with juice, some of the tomatoes could stand the engorgement no longer and split down the side, right there on the vine. They sparkled like Christmas lights in shades of gold, carmine, and lemon yellow. My kids selected them with more deliberation than treasures at a taffy store, and the treats rarely made it back into the kitchen.

After we'd arrive home with our CSA bounty, I'd spread the items out on the kitchen island. We would gather around to smell, touch, talk, admire, and praise the leafy greens, funny-shaped potatoes, or brussels sprouts still attached to the stalk. Sometimes I would pull a bouquet of greens up to my nose, give them a deep yoga inhale, and just live within the scent of cilantro or scallions. The squash could be so robust and voluptuous, I would pick them up and kiss their gnarly barnacled rinds in admiration. The berries—blue, black, or straw—we didn't discuss because they never made it further than the parking lot before they were evenly counted out and devoured. It made me want to say grace right then and there.

Unloading new varieties of food—and quite possibly ones you thought you didn't like—is a drawback for some first-time CSA members. For me, though, this was the best part. We were forced to experience, taste, and explore foods I wouldn't normally have purchased. It encouraged me to seek new cooking methods and try new recipes, as I had no idea how to cook garlic scapes or prepare celeriac. Slowly, I also had to embrace the habit of preserving food for later use and not complain at the abundance. I thought I would have to learn the almost forgotten art of canning so as not to waste buckets of tomatoes or bushels of summer squash, but I found freezing the surplus to be much easier.

The best advantage by far was that, by being a CSA member, I was no longer the vegetable villain. Since kale was provided in our share (I wasn't the one choosing it), my children no longer complained about being forced to try it. We looked at it as an adventure, all members of the same team. We moved from, "Here is your kale, go eat your dinner," to "We have kale today. What should we do with it? How do you like the kale compared to the chard?" Food became a family discussion—a bonus not spelled out in a membership fee.

Depending on your farm and CSA expectations, your family may have to volunteer on the farm a few times throughout the growing season. On our first ninety-minute assignment, we were on hands and knees harvesting potatoes. It was a steamy August morning, and it was tough with young kids who reached their attention span limits after twelve minutes. Working the land was much different from their household chores of feeding the dog or putting away dishes. Slowly, the grumbling gave way to immense pride and squeals of delight as tiny hands rummaged through the soft dirt unearthing treasures of potatoes. Call me crazy, but placing vegetables in a plastic sack from store shelves doesn't quite hold the same nostalgia as rooting around for your own dinner in the soil. The best part of our meal that evening was listening to their pride-filled voices, as they retold the day's adventure from their own perspectives.

I was fortunate Langwater Farm planted its first seeds on an eighty-eight acre historic property a half mile from my keyboard. Besides offering a fabulous farm stand of seasonal, local products, the best part was the farmers didn't believe in chemical farming.

Starting an organic farm must be a risky endeavor, since your future depends on the perfect amount of rain and sunshine to succeed. Being at the mercy of Mother Nature—including a late frost, a dry summer, or tomato blight—must be stressful work, to say nothing of the actual farming. Langwater's abundance of choices gently reminded me this had been the way of life for centuries. On my morning walks, I watched Kevin O'Dwyer, one of the farmers, turn the earth before planting. A broad-brimmed hat shaded his freckled skin and the twinkle in his eyes. The soil seemed to realize he was not there to demand or abuse it into submission, but to cultivate it with mutual respect. It was an important partnership; he must take care of the land if the land was to take care of him. Judging from the colorful selection and varieties of lettuces, radishes, beans, flowers, and squash I've purchased since their doors opened, Langwater Farm proves it is possible to grow food without the use of harmful chemicals. It does take a different approach and way of looking at things.

Bugs, for example, are not viewed as pests but as a challenge approached with creative solutions. Alida Cantor explained that their farm "supports a healthy ecosystem complete with birds, amphibians, mammals, worms, microorganisms, and insects." The robins that descend on the crops help control grubs, while swallows eat many of the flying insects that damage the foliage of fruits and vegetables. Toads also pull their weight and hop among the peas and beans looking for a tasty snack. Langwater Farm also protects against insect damage by covering certain crops with row cover—an opaque fabric tunnel that sits above the ground, letting light through while keeping bugs out.

Cantor has an amazing ability to teach, explaining to me how their farm kept the soil healthy and ready for growing crops without using synthetic fertilizers. "Cover crops are crops that are planted not to feed farm stand visitors but rather, to feed the soil. Continuously planting into a piece of ground will drain the soil's fertility, and since we are not adding high-nitrogen synthetic fertilizers, we need to keep a close eye on our soil fertility. Additionally, bare soil is prone to erosion. By covering our soil with cover crops even when we are not growing edibles, we can keep our valuable topsoil from being washed or blown away."

Pointing to the rows of turned dirt she continued, "Before we plant our spring crops, we till the cover crops back into the ground. They decompose, essentially forming a giant compost pile, adding valuable nutrients like nitrogen, and improving the soil structure by adding organic matter."

It made sense, but it was hard to wrap my brain around. My efficiency-focused mind scoffed at the thought of land sitting unused. Wasn't that a waste of money and resources? Cantor assured me that more wasn't always better. "By rotating areas of land in and out of production, we can ensure long-term soil health. All of this might seem like a lot of work for plants we aren't going to eat. But if we are going to keep harvesting bountiful food crops, it is essential to take good care of our soil."

For me, understanding the techniques used to farm without chemicals opened my mind. I'll never be a farmer in this life, but I relished the feeling that organic farming was possible. We didn't have to use synthetic chemicals to produce food. Cover crops, clays, compost, and fermented fish were used in harmony with a community of critters without having to worry about chemical runoff into the neighboring pond or the depletion of the bluebirds.

I was ecstatic to learn that not only did using organic farming methods eliminate chemical pesticides, but in one proud swoop, it removed synthetic fertilizers, radiation used on food, sewage sludge,* and synthetic preservatives from the picture. Subjects I could cross off my list! Terms I didn't need to research! By focusing on organic farming, I was left with simple, genuine farm food.

Lessons I learned from my CSA have carried over to my grocery store purchases. There is a rhythm in the seasons, and saving money on organic foods follows the calendar. For optimum prices as well as flavor, the mantra to remember is to buy in season, buy in bulk, and buy local. Just like my previous shopping habits, if I find a deal and it can be frozen or stored, then I bulk up. I have found organic whole carrots cheaper than conventionally grown prepared carrots. I frequently purchase five-pound bags and peel them while assisting my children during homework hour. Some I slice in the food processor and freeze in two-cup quantities for future soups and side dishes. Others I slice and put into cold water to supplement weekly lunches and ready-made snacks. I use my frozen corn, bell peppers, tomatoes, and fruits, in soups and smoothies all winter.

One season as a CSA member revolutionized the way my family ate and approached food. From a mom who reluctantly went on a quest to simply find pesticide-free veggies, I came away with more benefits

---

* Sewage sludge is a solid, semi-solid, or liquid residue leftover from domestic sewage treatment facilities. It can be repurposed and used as fertilizer on commercially grown food crops. Ewww.

than I could have ever imagined. I know I am providing more than safe, nutritious food for my children and family; I have planted seeds in their heads about food and its value and place in our lives. Salads don't just appear on our plate; veggies don't form on grocery store shelves overnight. The process of growing food responsibly takes a lot of hard work and effort. Our experiences discussing what we eat and working to put it on the table has changed how my family views food. It's not simply to fill us up and make us happy but is part of an intertwined system of respect for the land and future. It isn't always easy, but it is possible. I am quite hopeful that when my children become adults, they will crave genuine food. Well, the seeds are planted anyway. I can't guarantee they will sprout, but all factors considered, success is on my side.

Meaty Love Story

During the dance of our pre-engagement dating ritual, my husband shared many new aspects of the world I hadn't experienced before. Like a proud peacock, he introduced me to Major League Baseball, Pai Gow poker, clams in butter, and how to hit a bucket of balls at the driving range. Strutting his potential-husband skills, Ted wooed me by cooking his signature dish, creamy stroganoff, fresh from a sixty-nine cent spice packet. For our first Valentine's Day, I made him a dish of Lover's Spicy Kung Pao chicken. Of course, it was just plain ol' Kung Pao chicken, but enhancing the title elevated the mood for the evening. On drizzly weekends, we would snuggle on the couch to cheer on newcomer Alex Rodriquez of the Seattle Mariners, holding our mutually favorite bowls of white chicken chili. Until we met, I didn't realize how much childhood food preferences influenced the human mating ritual.

I was dating a Wyoming boy who loved country music and red meat. I took a liking to Garth Brooks and served meat because, well, I was a pleaser. I was more of a summer-fruit-salad-with-poppy-seed-dressing kind of woman. I wasn't quite a vegetarian. As a kid, I'd eaten my fill of tender Swiss steak cooked in an expanding oven bag along with our family heirloom recipe affectionately referred to as Yuck. It was a complex dish of tator tots layered with ground beef and frosted with a thick deposit of condensed cream soup. Not exactly a culinary masterpiece. My mom, a single mother, put in exceptionally long hours at work to raise my brother and me. Quick, three-step casseroles were staples.

Now that I was dating a meat lover, I tore pages from *Cooking Light* magazine, planned meals, and failed miserably. I would stare at slabs of red meat behind the butcher case, not knowing the difference between a loin, shank, or flank. I didn't enjoy cooking meat. I didn't like the smell of the flesh or having to responsibly consume the leftovers for the rest of the week. My man upped the ante. Not only did he enjoy pork chops, steaks, ribs, and beer braised brats, he was a hunter and opened my eyes to the literal meaning of bringing home the bacon. The nostalgia of hunting elk, deer, and pheasants meant more than just food to him. It was time he spent outdoors with his dad and had bow and arrow adventures with buddies. It was a respect for wildlife and knowing where his food came from—the actual sage-covered, high desert ravine in which the animals grazed. I could certainly meet him halfway and be open minded about my Rocky Mountain man's affinity for meat.

Back in the days when Ted and I could whisk away for the weekend, we spent some time in the amiable, all-American town of Scobey, Montana—a little dot south of the Canadian border. With my set of thermals, flannel jacket, and secret hopes of romance, I was ready for whatever the weekend had in store for me. Ted introduced me to family friends, whose open arms and kind hearts made me feel right at home on the ranch. One evening, catch-your-own pheasant was on the menu. It's one thing to pick your own lobster from a tank or fish from the pier hoping to snag a tasty ocean nibble for dinner, but sporting a loaded gun hoping to shoot a bird is quite another. We laced up our boots and went for a long walk beneath Montana's big sky grocery store, scouting for signs of pheasant. Afraid to let my inner sissy show, I walked alongside, observed, and took my share of razzing, but I didn't pull any triggers. A little while into the excursion, a gang of these gorgeous birds, flushed from the thigh-high grasses and shot down, lay crooked and limp on the

Earth. It was then I learned that the glamorous purse-sized pockets on his borrowed hunting jacket I was wearing had a purpose—for me to carry the still-warm birds, as we continued onward in search of what I hoped was the side salad.

We are humans. Many of us eat meat. If I had been born a few generations earlier, this pheasant experience wouldn't have been a courtship test but a commonplace chore. Plucking feathers from a Henny Penny carcass was a mundane, frequently performed ritual some time ago, probably similar to ripping open powdered cheese and boiling pasta today. While I tried to be open-minded about the hunting and meat-loving tendencies, killing my own dinner just wasn't going to become a part of who I was. I admit, I was much less help the rest of the weekend as the family worked together, laughing and talking, while our host's frozen steer was ground into winter's meatballs. When it came down to it, I was more mall girl than rancher, and the teenager in me stood to the side, wide-eyed with thoughts of, *Oh my Gawd. This is like, so totally grody.*

What we eat is deeply personal for us omnivores. How we were raised, our traditions, our family recipes, our worldview, and maybe even our religion, all shape how we eat and what we choose to value in food. For some, the type of meat served for dinner is determined by what lives in the woods, such as venison. For others, it is determined by what is shipped to us, like buffalo meat or Pacific Northwest salmon. While we have an awareness that what is on our plate was once alive, it is also a choice to understand the conditions in which it was raised. As a newlywed, I used a folder of magazine recipes and weekly sales flyers to determine the weekly meal plan. This method was easy and allowed me to put dinner on the table for many years. But now, I was learning there was more to food than met the eye; that it mattered how fruits, vegetables, or meats were grown and raised. I wanted to find a balance for my family—a way to tolerate and embrace meat (that I didn't have to hunt or raise myself) out of respect for my husband and children. After tackling the produce drawers in my fridge, I was now on the hunt for good-for-us meat.

Urban Hunter

Now, I headed out on a Kristi-style hunt—swapping the loaded weapon for my semi-automatic pocketbook—to determine if our meatballs, tacos, nuggets, and ham sandwiches were marinated in chemicals. I was elated at our fruit and veggies lifestyle enhancement, and I hoped to find comparable choices for my meat products. I had no idea where to begin, and my purse did not have deep pockets. Reading the meat packaging labels wasn't particularly helpful, as they didn't list medicinal antibiotics or growth hormones the animal had received. I suppose attaching an animal's vaccination chart to pre-formed burger patties wouldn't exactly be positive marketing, but it would have been useful. I had to go outside the nutritional label, beyond the Styrofoam base and plastic wrap, and begin with what the animal ate.

With produce, I didn't have to distinguish between insecticides used versus herbicides applied; choosing organic simply took care of all the implications. Was it the same with meat? Staring at the chuck roasts and chicken breasts in the mainstream meat department, there was no way for me to know what the animals had eaten. I didn't know if pesticides, herbicides, or fungicides were sprayed on the grain or grass consumed by a particular animal. Did pesticides from cow-food move from pasture to cud to dinner plate? Did they dissipate into avian flatulence? Did fungicides continue their travels into fatty tissue and become part of my pound of ground round? Since this information was beyond my control (and honestly, there was no real way for me to know the details), I was left with one starting point: no pesticides in the feed of the animals I purchased. This was the option I chose to pursue.

Unlike Bessie the cow from my Scobey, Montana visit, most mainstream meats are raised on factory farms. Factory farms started to develop in the early twentieth century as many grazing animals lost their traditional pastureland, with the focus shifting to crop yields and mass production. When the pastureland was taken over by productive corn crops, there was a need to raise and feed the animals but a lot less space in which to do it. CAFOs, or Concentrated Animal Feeding Operations, focus on raising meat as quickly and cheaply as possible. Cows, pigs, chickens, and turkeys live tightly confined in pens with little room for natural movement. Some animals, such as poultry, are provided with little or no access to sunlight or fresh air. Many of these animals are packed so tightly together, they live their entire lives standing in their own waste.

In my childhood days, when my family drove south of Sacramento, a familiar landmark was a cattle-feeding operation. It was always a chilling site: thousands of cows standing hoof-deep in prairies of sludge. I do not remember if my parents told me the animals were there to become fattened and slaughtered or not. We kids were too busy moaning in the back of the station wagon about the urine and manure stench that infiltrated the car and stayed with us for miles. Although my adolescent mind observed this morbid landscape with distaste, I had assumed it was just part of life. Little did I know what was happening behind the scenes of that cattle operation, as my family headed toward our latest vacation destination. According to the World Farm Animal Day website,

> Each year, ten billion cows, pigs, chickens, sheep, and other innocent, sentient animals are caged, crowded, deprived, drugged, mutilated, and manhandled in United States factory farms. They are then hauled to the slaughterhouse and killed under atrocious conditions. Nine percent (over 850 million) never make it to the slaughterhouse, dying from stress-induced diseases or injuries.[60]

For meat, the process of raising more animals in a shorter amount of time is tightly intertwined with living conditions. My own animal instincts rise simply by vacationing for a week with my family. Put all five of us in a one-bedroom hotel, and one of us is sure to melt down within the first three days (if not by the end of day one). My coping mechanisms to deal with stress are to grind my teeth, sigh, count to ten, and hope I don't lash out at my family. While my children like to think they are in charge and try to challenge the hierarchy of power with a dose of sibling rivalry, my firm maternal voice establishes the pecking order in my home. Similarly, throw a few thousand birds together for a short and (not so) sweet life and, well, they'll have trouble establishing their innate desire for a pecking order. They might not have teeth to grind, but they do have beaks to use as weapons. Normally sweet, curious birds, they turn to peck and injure each other when stressed or trying to establish the chicken-in-charge. In order to thwart this behavior, a popular practice in many chicken houses is to debeak the birds, cutting off a third of the top bill and the tip of the lower bill. When little pigs are bored or under stressful conditions, they bite each other's tails. The answer? A standard practice to tail-dock newborns. And those sows who want to make a mess of their pasture with their behavioral need to root? Nose rings will solve that problem. We are manipulating and altering animals for our economic gain. These are some of the side effects of our quest for massive meat production.

In an unfortunate cycle, we moved cows off pastures so we could grow chemically farmed corn and other government-subsidized crops. One of the uses for corn crops is to feed it to cows in feedlots. Now, a cow doesn't normally eat corn, it eats grasses. With no upper front teeth, adept cow tongues evolved to reach around and pull grasses. The grass slides down to the uniquely developed four-chambered stomach designed to process pastureland meals. Replacing green grasses with chemically raised corn allows the cow to be fattened and ready for slaughter in a mere twelve to thirteen months. If that cow was raised with an old-fashioned, cow-like life, grazing on pastureland the way nature intended, it would take a couple of years[61] before it would be ready to grill, roast, or fry.

What is the result when creatures are fed unvaried diets, have limited exercise, and are crowded together? They become unhealthy, obese, and diseased. The only way to combat the spread of disease among these animals is to use an arsenal of antibiotics season after season. The most recent FDA data shows that animals raised in the United States consume approximately 30.6 million pounds of antibiotics[62], with farm animals consuming approximately seventy-four percent of antibiotics used in the nation.

For most of my life, I naively believed giving antibiotics to animals was necessary for preventing disease. This is true if we insist on them living in unsanitary and crowded conditions. Animals with freedom to roam, fresh air to breathe, and space to turn and stretch don't need antibiotics to stay healthy. There are also some suggestions that overusing antibiotics have made those same medicines less effective. The bacteria that causes some diseases evolves at an accelerated rate just to stay alive, resulting in new strains of bacteria resistant to existing antibiotics and a population that is increasingly vulnerable to the new bacteria.[63]

The factory-farmed animal of today is evidently not the same as the farm animal of yesteryear. As an animal's lifestyle changes, its body changes as well. Just like us. If I were a mail carrier and packed my own lunch every day, then suddenly switched to sitting in an office chair eating fast food for lunch instead, my body shape would change. My tushie has become cushier just writing this book for the past year. It is easy to understand how our more-bigger-faster mentality has produced animals that are now physically different than they were just thirty years ago. Stephen Perrine, author of *The New American Diet*, shares, "We have changed the molecular structure of our beef and other protein sources." The chickens we raise now have an average of sixty-three percent as much protein and two-hundred-twenty-three percent more fat as the chickens served thirty years ago.[64] When our beef built its body out of natural grasses, we "ate a diet with an omega-3 to omega-6 ratio of 1:1." Now, the American diet has a ratio of closer to 1:20, and our body and brain are lacking this needed healthy fat. "When we cut costs in the name of production, we are cutting out the very benefits of the food our bodies are craving." One analogy from *The New American Diet* leaves me chuckling uncomfortably.

> To bring this all home, just imagine you were in a terrible plane crash in the Andes, like those poor souls in that movie *Alive*. And the only way to survive was to pick one of the dead folks to eat. And you had the choice of an obese, grotesquely muscled

offensive lineman for the Minnesota Vikings with shrunken testicles, who had been injecting himself with hormones for the past dozen years, or you could eat somebody else, someone of normal size and body type and hormonal function. Who would you choose? Well, every time you eat conventionally raised beef, you're choosing the Viking.[65]

Must we endure all these side effects of the meat processing industry for our Friday night cookouts and chicken salad sandwiches? No. In preparing it for my family, it was important to me that the animals had lived a decent life. So I set my sights on animals that generally had access to sun, movement, natural space, healthy living conditions, and organic food sources. I had finally found direction. For me, there was no compromise. I wanted the healthiest possible food for my family and not at the animal's expense of quality of life. I realized I didn't have to become a lover of top sirloin, and my husband didn't have to embrace piles of leafy greens. Deciding to simply purchase healthy, happy meat, could embrace both lifestyles. Of course, philosophy was one thing. Making it work was another.

I asked many meat department butchers if they offered any meat that had lived a happy life or if they knew how the meat had been raised. Most didn't know or have the answer for me. When I asked where the meat came from, they would point to a drawing of a pig or cow, indicating its shoulder or rump. Unfortunately, most meats in mainstream grocery stores are from animals raised in CAFOs. Trying not to become overwhelmed, I poked some fun and placed a want ad in one of my Be Choosy newsletters, mocking my desperation:

Seeking Evening Companionship

Can you satisfy my yearning for crock-pot rendezvous, spicy tacos, and steaming hot spaghetti sauces on cold winter nights? I am searching for a long-term relationship with grass-fed, organic beef to provide endless happy dinners for five.

I am fed up with bringing home deceptive groceries, possibly hiding unwanted antibiotics, pesticides, and hormones. Can I rekindle my love, trust, and simple enjoyment with quality, happy meat? Is it possible you are out there, not overpriced? Do you exist?

Signed,

Ima B. Leever

Romance at the Meat Counter

With no one replying to my want ad, I headed out on my own. While shopping at my local Whole Foods market, a grocery store dedicated to "selling the highest quality natural and organic products," I rounded the grocery aisle between dairy and seafood and gasped at what I saw in the meat section. With giddy excitement, I thought perhaps I might have found my soul meat.

To be fair, I'm a little dreamy when shopping at Whole Foods. The first national chain store to blend the natural foods industry into a mainstream supermarket format makes me tingle. My experience shopping there is a blend of back-to-school anticipation, four-year-old Disneyland euphoria, and maybe a couple fluttering jazz hands rolled into eighty-seven minutes and one overflowing cart. You see, for me, it's the only place tucked up here in the Northeast corner of our country that offers a selection of foods free from artificial preservatives, colors, flavors, sweeteners, and hydrogenated fats all in one location. While I can (and do) go searching hither and yon for healthy food options for my family, I'm as busy as the next mom. One-stop shopping is always a bonus.

Displayed in the Whole Foods meat case was a new, innovative, color-coded meat rating system. This visual technique allowed customers to understand, in just a glance, how the meat was raised. It proved to be a good first step for me in figuring out where my meat originated and the life it led before it came to reside behind the glass case. This five-step rating system was established by the Global Animal Partnership (GAP). This organization uses third party certifiers to evaluate the animals' health, well-being, handling, living conditions, and transportation. The findings were neatly categorized using brightly colored bars and touted the positives in shopper-friendly phrases:

Step 1: Orange = No Cages, No Crowding
Step 2: Orange Plus = Enriched Environment
Step 3: Yellow = Enhanced Outdoor Access
Step 4: Green = Pasture Centered
Step 5: Green = Animal Centered, Bred for Outdoors
And, a bonus Step 5: Green Plus = Animal Centered, Entire Life on Same Farm

Selecting a green over orange could be the difference between your Coq Au Vin having a place to perch and access to outdoor shade, versus living indoors full-time. Or the difference between your beef taking a twenty-five hour versus eight-hour ride from the farm to slaughter. GAP rated meat isn't exclusive to Whole Foods, but that's the easiest place to find it. In a glance, it allows the consumer a chance to make a more informed decision. An opportunity to choose wiser.

Another option within Whole Foods and some other traditional grocery stores is USDA Organic. USDA Organic promotes healthy, humanely treated animals by ensuring farmers provide them with organically grown feed and access to fresh air and the outdoors. It prohibits the use of antibiotics or added growth hormones. USDA Organic's ideals are a starting place when shopping at your favorite grocery store. Not all markets carry USDA Organic meat, however, and it can be a somewhat pricey option.

A third option has grown over the last few years as well: meat labeled Certified Humane®. The Humane Farm and Animal Care (HFAC) is a national nonprofit organization dedicated to improving the welfare of farm animals from birth through slaughter. When a product is labeled Certified Humane®, it meets HFAC program standards, which include a nutritious diet without antibiotics or hormones and animals raised with shelter and resting areas, sufficient space, and the ability to engage in natural behaviors. Certified Humane® rates meats, deli meats, dairy, frozen foods, and eggs. The standards for HFAC animal care are rigorous and fiercely protective of the animal's lifestyle. The drawback (for me) for Certified Humane® products is that animals don't have to be fed an organic diet. At this time, even though they are growing, it is also harder to find in mainstream stores. USDA Organic, GAP, and Certified Humane® are separate ideas, goals, and missions, toward the same movement. These organizations offer options and starting points for consumers who want healthier meat.

Out of my desire to stay on top of the latest meaty news, I registered for updates from HFAC. Occasionally an announcement will arrive in my inbox of a business who has recently (and proudly) earned the Certified Humane® label. When I receive these announcements, I take a moment to send the business a congratulatory email on their achievement. Regardless of whether they are local or not, I hope sending a random-act-of kindness note shows my appreciation for their efforts.

By taking this as a personal challenge, I was able to locate alternatives to grocery store CAFO meat. While I felt so much better about these choices, it meant cutting back on portions and accepting top prices. Then came my breakthrough. Our family visited a grass-fed cattle farm in western Massachusetts. A humble farmhouse overlooked rolling, pastured hills. We spent the afternoon talking to the farmers and touring the farm. There wasn't a stench. The Belted Galloway herd wasn't packed in confined spaces for profit. Pleased with what I saw and how I felt meeting the farmers who raised the cows, we purchased one hundred pounds of beef at $6.49 a pound. I know what you're thinking: "What everyday family has $650.00 to drop on a side of cow?" or "That's more than my car payment!" While it was more expensive compared to conventional grocery store ground beef, this was close to a year's supply of meat for us, simply paid up front. The best news? This delivery included T-bones, ribs, tenderloin, roasts, sausage, and stew meat—a steal by any grocery store flyer. Returning home, we divided the beef and cost among friends.* Purchasing meat this way does require a shift in shopping strategy, and finding friends to share the loot makes it more affordable for everyone.

Finding our grass-fed beef supplier was the solution to my meat search. I felt like I was doing something good for my family, beneficial, not just fulfilling a task. With a sigh of relief, I was delighted my burgers and sausage exceeded my hunter-husband's expectations for flavor and taste. Since cooking with grass-fed beef requires lower cooking temperatures and a third less time (due to less fat), once I mastered my techniques, I was set. Recipes that used slow- cooking methods were exceptionally succulent.

The most radical suppertime change was an emotional shift. I became deeply thankful. Maybe it was because I had invested so much time into the learning curve. Or maybe I felt at peace with nourishing my body with an animal that also had a decent life. Or maybe it was the extra money I was investing. Roast servings were smaller and bites savored. I made more of an effort to turn leftover chicken breast into chicken salad sandwiches for the next day's lunches. Poultry carcasses were turned into soup stock. Regardless, not a scrap was wasted or tossed into the garbage. We may spend a little more, but we use less, and enjoy deeply. None of us has ever craved unhappy, run-of-the-mill meat. Of course, Michael Pollan was able to capture many of my sentiments in *Omnivore's Dilemma*:

> The industrialization—and brutalization—of animals in America is a relatively new, evitable, and local phenomenon: No other country raises and slaughters its food animals quite

---

* Looking for grass-fed, local meat? Try starting at www.EatWild.com.

as intensively or as brutally as we do. No other people in history have lived at quite so great a remove from animals they eat. Were the walls of our meat industry to become transparent, literally or even figuratively, we would not long continue to raise, kill, and eat animals the way we do. Tail docking and sow crates and beak clipping would disappear overnight, and the days of slaughtering four hundred head of cattle an hour would promptly come to an end—for who could stand the sight? Yes, meat would get more expensive. We'd probably eat a lot less of it too, but maybe when we did eat animals, we'd eat them with the consciousness, ceremony and respect they deserve.[66]

Eggcellent Adventure

With produce and meat checked off, eggs moved their way up my list of items to tackle. I found myself frequently staring at the ovums in the four-by-eight refrigerated section of the grocery store. I had an affection for eggs, though our family did not consume them in large quantities. Their matte colors were serene, calming. Their shape was gorgeous, plump, and voluptuous. Their immensely strong frame cradled origin-of-life mysteries. You might say I had ovary envy, even though my admiration started long before my oophorectomy. Years ago, as an oil painter, I loved to attempt to capture their flawless form onto canvas. Now, amidst a wave of cold air, I stood between frozen cookie dough bricks and artificially colored yogurt trying to decide which specimens to take home.

White, brown, or green. *Which color would taste better?*

Cage free, free range, or free roaming. *Eggs roam?*

Omega-three infused or antibiotic free. *Promises, promises.*

What about this "vegetarian fed" label? Did that mean a vegan farmer was dishing up the chicken's dinner? How could hens be vegetarian when they scratched in the dirt for bugs and chased white winged moths for dessert? The features listed on carton labels were staggering. What a difficult life hens must have these days!

As I stood undecided and confused about which eggs to choose, my mental reinforcements tried to assist my decision making. A deep-voiced devil jumped onto my right shoulder and instructed with militant demand, *Buckle up soldier. You are the Secretary of Household Expense. Now, before your daughter tries to unbuckle and climb out of the cart, compare the per egg price between the six, twelve, and eighteen packages!* (Sure, this voice is a bit bossy, but it's the get-the-job-done part of me.)

Then, on my left shoulder, a gentler voice full of maternal wisdom whispered in my ear, *You are peaceful, mindful, and a steward of the earth. Look within, and you shall find the answer to Styrofoam, plastic, or cardboard cartons.* (I know, this part of me is a bit ethereal, but I like to imagine she's my sexy side with a tiny, glittery wand.)

It turns out, the USDA Organic eggs were the best option available in the grocery store. The mama hens of these eggs hadn't received any antibiotics or growth hormones (in the United States, poultry doesn't receive additional growth hormones), and they did not eat chemically farmed food. Their boutique, high-end price made them easy to spot. I begrudgingly paid for them. By now, I understood convenience had a price, and at the time, it was a place to start.

Now that I had my egg-dar on, I became aware of homemade signs stuck in front yards. Here were families raising small flocks of chickens, selling the extra eggs lemonade-stand style at clearance sale prices. While they weren't USDA Certified, I could get to know my egg farmer/hobbyist. I could see how the birds lived. It seemed odd, to not have a farm but to have farm animals in the middle of a neighborhood, but it got me thinking. Would chickens make it in our backyard? Wouldn't they attract coyotes that hunted in our woods? Or the darting red fox? Or the legendary clawed fisher cat who roamed at dawn? No, we certainly couldn't raise hens. A family of falcons lives just beyond our one-acre lot. Each year they glide above our yard, teaching their teenagers to fly, occasionally returning to their nest with a snake in their talons. (Yes, a happy snake.) Would they use my theoretical free-roaming hens for target practice? No, we certainly couldn't have chickens.

Except... maybe... well, wouldn't it be fun? Wouldn't having our own backyard chickens be a memorable experience, you know, for the kids? My husband didn't think so. It would be odd to own chickens in a neighborhood development. I let the idea simmer with him. Tick tick tick. Sometimes I have to grab the wheel and steer my own ship. Soon enough, the phone rang. "Mrs. Marsh? This is the Easton Postmaster. We have a package here for you. And it's peeping." Well, if my husband hadn't been on board before, now was his chance to jump on the ship. Especially considering the ship had arrived peeping, and I couldn't send it back.

Kaytee and I zipped to the post office where they handed us a small, insulated box with air holes. The chicks had been born the day before, the nutrients from the egg still in their tummies. They had less than twenty-four hours to be shipped safely to our home. Excitedly, we opened the box and peered in. Five, fuzzy balls of feathers cried out: one auburn, one speckled, two soft gray, and one classic yellow. The line of parcel-carrying adults behind us gathered around to welcome Molly, Minnie, Becky, Jennie, and Shelly to Massachusetts.

We created a chicken nursery in our basement using a heat lamp and an old port-a-crib. Our newborns (or new-hatched) endured a constant parade of admiration from my children and visitors. Raising baby chicks infused another level of tenderness into my children. They would gently hold each fluff ball with cupped hands, the chick soon falling asleep from the warmth. Even Daisy, our bird-hunting Labrador, watched over them with the curiosity of Clifford the Big Red Dog, peering into the playpen netting. Kyle created a roosting area out of twigs and spent hours teaching each chick how to perch. I'm sure chicks innately learn to perch, but he was filled with parental pride similar to, "MY kid rode a bike with no training wheels at three-years-old," and his efforts paid off: our chickies learned to roost at an early age. I always knew they were exceptional little fluffs!

Refusing to let this be an expensive venture (the last thing my husband needed was economic reasons why chickens weren't a good idea), I headed outside armed with duct tape, a staple gun, and a butter knife intent on repurposing a neighbor's plastic playhouse into a chicken coop. This, of course, inspired my husband to rescue our backyard from looking like a potential dump site under my architectural direction. I'm no idiot. I know if I want something done, I need to do it myself, or at least *look* like I'm going to do it myself. And what do you know? My husband offered to help create a loving home for our flock. Armed with a large roll of chicken wire, Ted and Kyle spent a long weekend building the coop. When the chickens turned three-months-old, we moved them into their own apartment with a future rent of thirty blue-green eggs a week.

Neighborhood kids flocked to our yard when we brought the hens out to roam in a small fenced area. The hens aerated our lawn with scratching, ate pesky bugs, and randomly fertilized the grass. They quickly reminded us they were birds after all, as they easily flew over the mobile fence. After escaping their playpen prison, they pecked and waddled around in pure bliss, always staying together in a clique. A chick clique, to be exact.

Raising and owning chickens turned out to be much easier than raising my own kids. After forgetting to put the hens away at night (more than once), we witnessed their nesting nature. At dusk, they would head into their coop, hop up onto the roosting branches, snuggle up together, and go to sleep without a single nag or plead from me. Why couldn't my children go to bed as easily? Just wander into their rooms at 8:30 p.m. (teeth already brushed), climb into bed, and fall soundly asleep? Why couldn't my kids be more like my chickens, at least in this area?

As time progressed, I liked my feathered family more and more. We began letting them out mid-morning, and they'd spend their days circling the house, never straying too far from home. On sunny days, I set aside my keyboard and sat on my bench to shift gears, soak in warm rays, and watch my Ladies. They too worshiped the sun. They would lie on their feathered sides in the dirt with one wing fanned and a long scaly leg extended like a 1940s calendar pin-up girl. They were intensely loyal to each other, and if one strayed, the others became ruffled and agitated until all were accounted for. They held private conversations with each other, their throaty "rrrrr"s sharing secrets I couldn't understand. They kept little Shelly, who was at the bottom of the pecking order, in line. As the only blonde Easter chick, she received a lot of human attention as a baby, and I think the others resented it.

It really wasn't too long ago when everyone had chickens, yet today they are an anomaly, odd and foreign. Many children came to my house wanting to know what kind of birds they were—not "is that a Rhode Island Red or a Barred Rock?"—but "what IS that?" These same kids could teach me about Epi-Pens, asthma inhalers, or which pretzel brand was allergy-friendly and could be shared at school, but they were a tad unfamiliar with a real, live chicken. Now I could show them how to pet one and search for a warm, fresh egg.

I'm surprised at how many adults don't understand how chickens lay eggs and frequently ask, "Don't the hens need a rooster?" Hens are much like women when it comes to eggs. Human women release an egg once a month. If we had, say, a rooster around, it is possible our egg would be fertilized and develop into a baby. Without a rooster around, hens are free to lay their eggs not monthly, but daily. Without fertilization, they do not become chicks, but breakfast. No rooster, no chick; no man, no baby. Just eggs all around. Some being better for scrambling, of course.

Looking out the kitchen window one afternoon, I witnessed my three children playing together good-naturedly and cheerfully. It was one of those divine mommy moments, watching my kids sitting criss-cross-applesauce on top of the picnic table, each snuggling a chicken in his or her lap. They were deep in conversation, possibly telling stories or sharing secrets never-to-be-discussed-with-Mom. They referred to this special time together as "chicken conversation." If I didn't already love these birds, this mere feat alone would have sealed the deal. Since coming into our lives, these birds provided our breakfast, put themselves to bed each night, and engendered warm feelings between brothers and sister. I have even heard my husband chatting away with the Ladies while he was doing yard work. If five birds could work this kind of magic, I silently wondered what effects seven would have on our family. Or nine?

Oh yes, their eggs were amazing as well! It's easy to get wrapped up in the social aspects of chicken rearing when you live with them every day, but I originally brought them home to provide my family with nutritious, free-range, happy eggs. (Friendship was an ancillary benefit, but certainly no less important.) People ask me, "Is a free-range farm egg really better than a conventional store-bought one? How much different can an egg taste?" They are looking for me to confirm their suspicions that there is no difference between the two, except price. If you've never eaten a freshly laid egg, it is difficult to make verbal comparisons. The taste is meaty, rich, and thick in a way difficult to describe unless it's on the end of your fork.

If you are what you eat, then the same goes for a hen and her eggs. Visually speaking, a farm fresh egg has a deep orange yolk, not the pale yellow most people are used to. This is because a free-range chicken egg contains nutrients from many sources: bugs, spiders, leaves, grass, worms, chicken feed, and the occasional treat supplied by owners. The eggs are meatier (say when slicing through one cooked over-medium), and deviled eggs have more flavor. The chicken's stress-free lifestyle, varied menu, and typically healthier living conditions all significantly contribute to a healthier-for-you egg.*

Free-range farm eggs have more nutritional benefits than conventionally produced ones. Compared to conventional eggs, pastured eggs have:

- 1/3 less cholesterol
- 1/4 less saturated fat
- 2/3 more vitamin A
- Two times more omega-3 fatty acids
- Three times more vitamin E
- Seven times more beta-carotene [67]

For those who say they can't taste the difference between the two, I say, one is still better for you, better for the chickens, and better for

---

* The grocery store eggs, on the other hand, come from hens that likely lived a life crammed into an 18x20 inch wire cage, sharing this space with five to eleven other hens. PETA describes, "280 million chickens used each year for their eggs, called 'laying hens' by the industry, endure a nightmare that lasts for two years. Even in the best-case scenario, each hen will spend the rest of her life crowded in a space about the size of a file drawer with four other hens, unable to lift even a single wing."

our planet. Those reasons alone make pastured eggs the choice for my family. Molly, Minnie, Becky, Jennie, and Shelly agree.

Got Hormones?

The second my children were born, I felt there was suddenly a huge emphasis placed on milk. I was advised that breast milk was best for proper growth. After breast milk came whole milk because growing toddlers needed the milk fat for continued brain development. As each of my children turned two, I waited for the green light to switch to skim, because they no longer needed the fat but still needed the calcium.

I've done my best to make sure my children got the calcium and dairy products they needed, spooning yogurt into them for breakfast, peeling wrappers off string cheese, and letting them indulge in the frequent drippy ice cream cone. But while researching our family food products, I came across a startling fact. Dairy farmers were injecting genetically engineered bovine growth hormones (rBGH or rBST) into cows to increase lactation. I was more upset to learn that the FDA approved the use of these growth hormones in 1993 and without asking dairy-lovers how they felt about it. It also wasn't just the milk that was affected but all products containing milk.

rBGH stimulates and increases lactation, which means a higher milk yield for dairy farms. A higher yield means more money for the farmer and the potential for cheaper milk. Who hasn't complained about paying almost $4.00 for a gallon of cow juice? Using hormones means more milk at cheaper prices. It all sounds very win-win, doesn't it?

Mama cows may find this to be one situation worth crying over spilled milk. That's because cows given rBGH experience higher rates of mastitis, a painful udder infection. I certainly can't relate to having my beak trimmed or my tail docked, but I have dealt with my share of swollen, infected, lactating boobs (from nursing, of course). The fever and flu-like symptoms from a localized mastitis infection relegated me to a weekend on the couch on more than one occasion. Any woman who has ever experienced this knows her breasts are so sore and tender, she doesn't even want people in the same *room* with her for fear they may accidentally brush against her inflamed chest, sending her into fits of swearing and tears. I have half the number of teats as a mama cow. If one infection is horribly painful, what must having three or four feel like? I certainly would have been swayed to modify my purchasing habits by simply hearing that giving cows growth hormones increases pus from infected udders. Naysayers might point out, I am not a cow and can't know how a cow feels, but I assume they aren't cows either. I appreciate the vote of confidence that I am not a bovine, but as a sister lactating mammal, I can empathize.

Surprisingly, that isn't the controversial side effect. Jeffrey Smith, my GMO mentor, shared more lessons about dairy products. "Milk from rBGH-treated cows has much higher levels of IGF-1."[68] This is a naturally occurring hormone in cows as well as humans. However, higher levels of this hormone have been linked to an increased risk of breast cancer[69] and other cancers. "IGF-1 levels in milk from cows treated with rBGH can be up to ten times higher." Many other industrialized countries, including Japan, Australia, New Zealand, and Canada[70] have banned the use of bovine growth hormones due to health risks to humans and harm to animals, even to the point that rBGH dairy products from America are not welcome or accepted in the European Union and Canada.

The good news, of course, is that there are choices. As a latecomer to the party, I could easily find milk and some milk products at the grocery store labeled *rBGH-Free* or *rBST-Free* or *No Hormones Added*. (You may find *hormone-free* labels, but some argue an animal product cannot be truly hormone-free because of the animal's natural hormones.) By choosing the next level of milk, USDA Organic, I was able to offer products to my family that did not contain growth hormones and had strict guidelines as to how the cow was raised and fed. An added bonus to my organic milk choice was that recent reports stated organic milk contained seventy percent more omega-3 fatty acids and fifty percent more vitamin E than regular milk.[71] The best news of all was that I found healthy milk options without having to build a barn for Bessie the cow next to the chicken coop. My husband was udderly thrilled.

Gluttonous Waist

Something about Texas air is sweet to me. With family tucked away in small towns, we visit often, and the fragrance from the earth and grasses resonates in me. During one trip to the Lone Star State, it was still winter at home, but there we were wearing tank tops with our cowboy boots. While my kids searched for roadrunners and armadillos, I talked with a rancher about the massive bovines on his acreage. They spent most of their lives out to pasture and seemed to enjoy their slow and peaceful existence. Near the end of their lives, they were transported to be finished off with corn. Watching them graze, I assumed their tank-like bodies, broad shoulders, and even wider horns made them clumsy and slow. I was curious if they were affectionate but was not about to scale the fence and approach one for a snuggle. Instead, I leaned on my side of the fence, choosing safety. Comfortable talking to the rancher, I asked why the cattle were topped off with corn before slaughter. In his easy-going "it's the way it is" manner, he told me it was because of demand. Finishing the cows off with corn decreased the number of days from birth to slaughter, allowing for more beef to be produced in a shorter amount of time. Without this process, demand would not be met. I was succumbing to his reasoning. Before the synthetic revolution, chemical farming, or CAFOs, only one billion humans had lunches to pack and dinners to serve. Two hundred tiny years later and in a world population spike, we are nearing seven billion bodies needing food. We were topping off cattle to speed up the process.

Whoa there, Nellie. Hold your thoughts. Demand? From *our* society? What exactly are we demanding? We certainly don't have a lack of beef, do we? Any trip to the grocery store reveals case upon case of fresh beef, frozen beef, and a myriad of beef products. Restaurants dole out super-sized, triple layered burgers and extra-large steaks. How much of this beef ends up in trash bins and landfills? Yes, I suppose the demand is there. We require cheaply produced corn and crops to feed the CAFO animals to meet our gluttonous demand, over-indulgence, and over consumption to the point of waste (or waist). Demand is out of control. We don't need statistics to point this out; America's problem with obesity makes it clear. For those of you who (like me) enjoy cold, hard facts to aid your digestion, the USDA had this to say about American food consumption:[72]

- Average daily caloric intake increased by 24.5%, or about 530 calories, between 1970 and 2000.
- The percentage of Americans who were overweight went up from forty-six percent in 1980 to sixty-two percent in 2000.
- The total average annual meat consumption increased fifty-seven pounds from the 1950s to 2000. Since this time, each American has consumed an annual average of seven pounds more red meat, forty-six pounds more poultry, and four pounds more fish and shellfish.

So yes, there are more of us, but we are eating much more as well. What about all the food we don't eat? When we go out for dinner, restaurants serve the super-sized platters that make us feel like we are getting a great value, but instead we pat our swollen bellies, loosen our belts, and push the plate away. That great value we thought we purchased is scraped into the garbage. My distaste for waste has been growing parallel to my increase in appreciation for food. Our per capita food waste has doubled since 1974. A conservative figure from Jonathan Bloom's *American Wasteland*: "160 billion pounds of food [is] squandered annually," more than enough to fill the Rose Bowl to the brim. A high-end estimate (of 295 billion pounds) would almost fill the Rose Bowl twice over. Bloom estimates that this amounts to an annual total of 197 pounds of discarded food per person each year.[73]

Then there is waste of another kind—when errors in our food system end in recalls. When hearing of the latest recall, my thought process, mumbled and jumbled, vacillated between, *How in the world do they track it?* to self-reassuring, *I'm pretty sure I don't buy that brand.* I can't fathom buying my child a hamburger only for him or her to get extremely sick the next day. The good news is, we can recall products. I was curious though—what happened to all those recalled items?

While searching around on the Internet, I came across the USDA Recall Case Archive. Initially I wanted to compile a decade's worth of recalls hoping to shock you with the amount of sheer waste. Turns out, I didn't need a decade's worth—just one year of recalled products was incomprehensible. A tidy table listed recalled items such as breaded chicken wings, teriyaki beef jerky, sautéed chicken, raw pork paste, ready-to-eat fried pork loaf, canned poultry products, ginger sausage, bison products, beef stroganoff, cheesy chicken, beef carcasses, and pork skin products. In 2010 alone, over 1,350,000 pounds of pork, cattle, turkey, and chicken were recovered. A negligible amount was attributed to non-meat products like vegetable pot stickers, and twenty-two more cases were not filed in the archive yet.

The products recovered for this particular year were for reasons including: items produced without inspection, under processed, contained foreign materials, mislabeling, misbranding, and items containing prohibited materials. (Like a farm boot or concealed weapon? What constituted a prohibited material?)

This was just in one year in the United States. Would someone tell me what 1.3 million pounds of animal-based food products looks like? Fifty pounds of ground beef just might fit into a decent sized roll-on suitcase. (I do buy our meat in bulk.) That would be 26,000 suitcases of food recalled and disposed of for just that year. Don't get me wrong, I am appreciative to have a detailed system to recall food (especially since we don't have one for personal care products) when there are undeclared allergens or salmonella found in what I was going to chop, dice, and serve. I find it disheartening that we have so much needless waste with so many human errors in the process.

So what kind of picture does our food system paint? We grow cheap corn and grain to feed and fatten our animals quickly, which we raise on farms geared for mass production, then we transport and slaughter those animals for food products, which we then scrape from our plates or recall from our store shelves. Our demand is gluttonous, our behavior irresponsible, and our health is at risk.

Judgment Day

For my family, there was a major difference between changing over our personal care products and changing over our food. With personal care products, I could swap out a toothpaste brand and ruffle very few family feathers—just place it on the counter and deal with minimal conversation. Hammering out how and where to buy happy bacon, eggs, and cantaloupe required patience. Molding my family into genuine-avores (Why isn't there a word that means "genuine food eater?") required an entirely different approach. Serving a sumptuous meal was not the obstacle. The overwhelming outside influences of the world my kids lived in threatened to bury my message. At times, it felt like a reality show of Me versus The World. The apprehension of what these changes would mean for my children's long-term emotional health left me feeling worried. Gaining my family's buy-in required chipper, upbeat, infomercial sales skills that were occasionally difficult to muster. I forged ahead anyway, knowing that ultimately, I was doing the right thing.

Turns out, the most arduous obstacle wasn't coercing my husband to build a chicken coop under our deck. We owned all the tools, hanging neatly in the garage on pegboard, although I thought they were just for show. It wasn't the statewide hunt for happy hamburger patties or learning how to make pizza sauce from August's bounty of tomatoes. The most disheartening task then (and now) was maneuvering through the relentless bombardment from the outside world designed to entice my children into believing junk food is the norm.

After everything I unearthed during my research, I understood the world did not have my family's health in its best interest. Constantly trying to shield them was exhausting. Modern parenting felt like pushing a double stroller through the Boston Marathon in a hailstorm while trying to protect the kiddos amidst a constant barrage of pelting, frozen peas.

I first sensed this dark cloud when Tanner entered preschool. I was delighted for his first taste of independence and ninety minutes in a loving, nurturing environment. However, I silently observed the parent-supplied, non-birthday cupcakes twice the size of his pudgy fist, handed out for 10:00 a.m. snack. As a relatively new mom, I hadn't found my voice. I kept my opinions to myself and rarely stood up for what I thought. Unspoken mom-pressure kept it that way. Instead, I watched the children's eager eyes and giddy smiles as the "favorite moms" brought in frosted delights and the disappointment on their faces when I provided sliced apples and pretzel sticks.

When my second son, Kyle, entered school, he brought home a memo outlining allowable, allergy-friendly snacks. The "healthy food" column included Twizzler candy and marshmallows. Just what my kids needed—a printed document from the educational system classifying blown sugar as a recommended health food. Since then, our schools have made progress and now support and encourage healthier snacks. But that experience was an eye-opening parenting lesson for me; regardless of my personal philosophies and preferences, I couldn't control what happened outside my home.

As errands and afterschool activities increased with age, the constant, cheap junk food confrontations went from pea-sized pelts to a frozen strawberry pounding. At the grocery store, I fended off well-intentioned bakers who offered my children pancake-sized frosted cookies while I shopped for bread. Those cookies were so pretty, so enticing, yet my firm, gentle voice asked, "Didn't you already have a treat in school?" While waiting in line for the cashier, we spent about seven tortuous minutes surrounded sneaker-to-pigtail by candy bars and bubble gum in the checkout lanes. Tired, battered, and grouchy, I curtly replied to every request, "No. Just no," while trying to choose between paper or plastic since my reusable bags were in the trunk. On Tuesday afternoons, we'd sit for thirty minutes in a musty, guitar-lesson lobby surrounded by a pile of year-old Popular Science magazines and two glaring vending machines which whispered, "Cheetos anyone? Coke? Snickers? Anyone? Anyone?" Like a *Groundhog Day* movie flashback, I kept repeating to my duckling entourage, "No, honey, not today." Pelt, pelt, pelt. Baseball practice involved two hours sitting on bleachers adjacent to a well-placed snack shack, the air saturated with the tantalizing aroma of fried dough, hot popcorn, and deep-fried chicken nuggets. Spring was damp and chilly and even I had to be strong. I'd chant, "We'll be home for dinner in an hour." School fundraisers kicked off in September with motivating pep rallies encouraging my children to sell frozen cookie dough or boxes of chocolate candy bars so their classes could win, of all things, an ice cream party. The barber handed out lollipops. The red candy machines on the way out of the toy store offered Skittles, Boston Baked Beans, and gumballs for a measly quarter. My children were constantly asking for quarters.

It really wasn't the isolated instances—the one friend who baked sumptuous brownies or the neighbor who invited my children to decorate egg-shaped sugar cookies—it was the exhaustion from battling the constant barrage of excess that depleted me. From the viewpoint of a person under forty-eight inches, the world was a Candyland—a couple Oompa-Loompas short of Willie Wonka's Chocolate Factory. We lived in a tantalizing, tempting, coaxing, persuading, junk food Garden of Eaten.

So whom did that make me? Let me tell you. Not a noble, admired, loved family member. Not the brownie baking, generous best friend (whose hostessing I truly did admire). It made me the No-Meister. No this. No that. No. No. No. A sour-party-pooper-wound-too-tight-mother. An evil mommy. A control freak. A woman who wanted to throw the towel in every three days, give or take a grocery trip. An exhausted parent who fell asleep wondering, *Was I even a good mom today? Did my kids feel any love from me? Did we laugh or talk?* I despised being Sergeant No.

At this point, it may surprise you to know I do encourage my kids (and even myself) to revel in life's pleasures. My weakness is salty, crunchy snacks and cheesy, warm appetizers at book club or at football parties.

I'm not embarrassed to admit that all members of the Marsh family have a love for cookies—homemade chocolate chip or oatmeal cookies to be exact. Instead of being a dictator, I found empathy by declaring, "My favorite cookies are oatmeal, especially warm from the oven!" My children were amazed I was, in fact, not a cold-hearted control freak, but a real human who also loved warm cookies. On occasional Sunday afternoons, I pull down our organic ingredients, and the kids mix and scoop. The Easter Bunny manages to bring treats, and Santa Claus still fills stockings. Birthdays have cakes. I am not such the Evil One.

While I embrace a special treat here and there, the definition of "treat" has become muddied. I have read that a treat used to be a juicy, seasonal fruit; the sweetness from a watermelon or blueberry was all we humans needed. (I wonder what the checkout aisles looked like then! Were children surrounded sneaker-to-pigtail in clementines and kumquats?) Did we once nibble on those items with the same reverence we now give to a chocolate-frosted donut? In many cases, treats simply blend in with everyday food. Which part of fast food is the treat: hamburger, fries, or soda? All of them? Or do we consider that dinner, and for a treat we order an additional apple pie or chocolate shake? If a food's first five ingredients include one or more types of sugar, shouldn't we consider that a treat of the week? This definition varies from parent to parent. We can't teach our children moderation without first deciding how we define a treat. Is it sweets? Junk food in general? When should we indulge? How often? What is a healthy rule of thumb? Do we look to books, or do we look within for our answers?

Defining a treat is also difficult for our children. On one particular trip to a discount store, I challenged my kids, "Buy any snack you want as long as it is healthy." (Interpretation: I will be as humanely patient as possible while waiting for you to make a decision in the name of a life experience, even if it takes you twenty minutes of perusing all the aisles.) I thought this was a rather generous exercise, as I did not start the sentence by setting a price limit or dictating what they could not have. At the end of the quest (and my patience), one of my children went for nuts. Another for raisins. And the third proudly decided on fruit...snacks, that is. Fruit snacks. Gummy, plastic snacks, made with nothing but recently invented corn syrup and food colorings (*not* genuine food). My son's long lashes and sky blue eyes melted with disappointment as he tried to grasp why this didn't pass. Why? They were called fruit (pointing at the illustration on the package). His friends ate them for *snacks*, not *treats*. Why was mom saying with a firm, clenched voice, "Let's choose something better"? In the end, it was eye opening to see the world from their level. Kids don't compare toothpaste, but they do compare lunch box items. They don't proudly share what brand of shampoo they use but are proud to announce what snacks or treats they brought from home. As soon as children hit the school cafeteria, they learn not-so-subtle messages about what food is cool to eat and what is not.

Another lesson started with a slamming door, a backpack thrown on the floor, and a beaming daughter exclaiming, "Mom we had Oreos for snack today at school!" Then she paused, reconsidered her words and whom she was telling. "They were *organic* Oreos." I bit my lip. I was silent. I looked at her. She was only six and she was trying to be aware of the things her mom was concerned about. Finally my restraint faltered, and I broke out laughing, causing a flash of anger to cross her face. "Honey, Oreos—organic or not—are *not* food." It made sense to me, as junk food does not equate to real food. *To me.* I had forgotten my audience, and my response brought utter confusion and watery eyes. Emphatically and assertively (I do love this in her) she stated, "Yes. They are. They have *wheat*." What could I say? The double-sided chocolate cookies, a precious treasure, were handed out by her beloved teachers and ravished by her peers. Who was I in her world? It will be a few more years before she really understands my selective, food classification system. In the meantime, I will bite my lip and celebrate her awareness instead. My children did want to show me they were doing their best, but again, many times I stumbled and had to learn as well.

With the lessons my children taught me, I dug down deep and decided to employ the strategies parents use to prepare their kids for social pressures—awareness and discussions—to arm my children with tools to navigate through real-life seductions. If we can empower children to face down cigarettes, drugs, underage drinking (and now what kind of lip-gloss to buy), I certainly could educate them around the dinner table, while shopping, or while traveling. My goal became to raise my children to be media savvy, with the confidence to resist peer pressure with a polite "no thank you" when needed, in hopes they would go forth and make decent decisions in the name of health and a good life.

I muster up my resolve, stand my ground, and offer bear hugs and an "I'm so proud of you!" for report cards and season-ending baseball games. The outside world offers prizes in boxes, social acceptance through brand names, and funny cartoon characters on packaging. My nemesis—junk food companies and their advertising—spent 4.2 million dollars in advertising in 2009.[74] That is some serious persuasion vying for my children's loyalty, birthday money, and lifelong addictions. I will never be bigger or more powerful than the industry. I can only do what I can do.

When I shifted to this viewpoint, I found tools ready and available for parents like me. Jamie Oliver's *Food Revolution* television series brought in someone other than Mom leading the discussion. The website, www.theMeatrix.com, used cartoon spoofs to share the basics of factory farming to a preteen's mind without using real animal film footage. Michael Pollan published his *Omnivore's Dilemma* in a young adult version, which I now recommend to most adults. *Food Inc*, a movie inspired by *Omnivore's Dilemma,* now stimulates peer discussion in high school philosophy classes as well as being an effective introduction tool for husbands. I was careful not to preach to my children. I empathized alongside them, discussing why it is harder in their generation than it was in mine. At least my age group simply didn't know. We discussed what it meant to farm organically and why some farmers chose to do it. I thought it would be better to feed them morsels of information, let the conversation develop, and allow their questions to guide the way. I resolved not only to answer them truthfully but also to be the best role model I could. I'm a firm believer that children learn more from what they watch and witness than what they hear. This, of course, meant I couldn't constantly indulge in my favorite snacks either. I, too, had to practice restraint and choose the apple or carrot sticks over the potato chips, even when I really, really wanted those chips. No more using the excuse, "Because I'm the mom," when my kids asked why I was allowed to do something they weren't. I believe if they witness that these ideals are important to me today, then these ideals will be important to them tomorrow.

Wake Up Call

Regardless of what my internal instinct professed and the many compromises I felt I made for my children, it was hard to shake one conversation that struck deep in my Achilles' heel. It had started innocently enough among girlfriends as we gathered at a local restaurant. We imbibed in our drinks of choice—margarita on the rocks with salt, a red wine, a lemon drop martini, and a glass of water—and noshed on a heaping plate of hold-the-unhappy-beef nachos with extra guacamole. Our conversations on these nights ran the gamut from upcoming summer vacation plans to the husband-problem-du jour. Tentatively, I divulged how I was exhausted by the breakfast cereal battle, fully aware even my friends might scoff at me. I complained that my genuine food outlook did not include the myriad combinations of layered sugars, processed corn, and preservatives. There were just better choices for breakfast, and I wanted to step it up. My children were used to stumbling down the stairs, mumbling, and slouching over their bowls of breakfast cereal while trying to wake up. My husband joined forces with the kids and agreed cereal was convenient. *Mutiny!* I thought. They banded together with dug in heels. "I tried to show them all the options. A toasted, whole-wheat bagel with peanut butter. Fruit. Oatmeal. Nuts. Leftovers! They wanted nothing of it. Maybe I am a bit stubborn," I conceded to my friends, searching for their "motherhood is hard" consolation.

Instead, roused chuckles and I-told-you-so looks sent me deeper into my pity phase. One friend replied, "My mom never gave us boxed cereals. Ever! And you know what? When I went away to college, I ate Cocoa Krispies every day!" Another chimed, "My parents were really strict about food. As soon as I had my own job and could finally eat like my friends, I ate out all the time. When I moved out, I gained thirty pounds in two years! I still haven't lost it. There is no way I will put a moratorium on food in my house." Their stories weren't pretty. Tales of adolescent and young-adult rebellion proliferated. Fabulous. Did I now have to add psychological well-being to my grocery shopping decision-making factors? Was it not enough to contemplate cost-nutrition-GMO-pesticides-cholesterol-sodium-sugar-coupons-sales-proximity-to-my-house and paper-versus-plastic? I also needed to calculate what my kids would share with a therapist? I drained my margarita and caught the attention of the cocktail server, indicating I'd like another. Make it a double.

My actions could send my children spiraling into rebellion. That unsettled me. Being an Evil Mommy was now the least of my worries. Real stories had voiced potential future outcomes. Would my children rebel? Would they hoard Ding Dongs and Girl Scout Cookies in their nightstands? Would they crack open a Dr. Pepper with their Cocoa Krispies for breakfast in their bachelor pads? Would crumpled fast food bags be tossed into the backseats as they ate, drove, and texted their way to the liquor store? It *would* be so much easier to go with the flow—to pretend I didn't know what I knew. Where did my virgin days of ignorance go? And why, again, did I give them up?

I was torn. With the thump of my ruling staff, I wanted to decry, "I *made* these kids! I clean these dishes! My kids! My house! My philosophy! I am Queen of my kitchen with ultimate control and protection over tiny bodies! No soda! No junk food! No slimy birthday party pizzas or ridiculous colored sports drinks! Ever!" Trumpets would play, and my royal wee-subjects would bow, curtsy, and gleefully eat peanut butter frosted celery sticks dotted with raisins. How I would love ruling Kristi-dom!

In reality, I was starting to understand there were limitations to the protection I could provide. I could be overzealous, or I could prepare them to be young adults. While overzealous was my knee-jerk reaction, thankfully my sanity and reason erred on the side of preparation.

I had to find my position on the parenting spectrum. With this decision, as with all the others parents make, there wasn't a right or wrong way, a black or white answer. Do we as parents discuss with our partners the choice between breast milk or formula? Ears pierced as toddlers or on thirteenth birthdays? We try to navigate the social pressures our children face by asking ourselves, "Am I the parent who will say zero beer in the house? Should I hide the beer we have? Should we leave the beer out and let kids learn its place in our world but instruct that it's off limits to them? Should I be the cool parent who throws the underage kegger because the kids are bound to drink somewhere, it might as well be at home?" With each decision comes a reaction. By limiting treats or offering sweets, will I encourage a future addiction? By talking through real world challenges or condemning them, will I empower health or send them on a path toward inevitable liver disease? Finding our own answers along the food journey is an enormous battle.

My own answer came to this: I have three, amazing human beings bestowed on me, and yes, they are my responsibility. They have eighteen years under my influence (arguably maybe only twelve), but this time is critical for many things: bone growth, reproductive development, brain formation, and proliferation of healthy breast cells, just to name a few. In addition, I do not know if any of us will be here tomorrow or in five years. So when it comes down to it, whether it's one hundred and twenty years, or slightly less, it is my job to encourage these bodies to breathe fully, play hard, appreciate deeply, and love intensely. I echo this to my children gently and often: "This isn't easy for me either. If I didn't

145

help you learn and help you love your bodies, I wouldn't be doing my job."

Make It Fun and It Will Get Done

A rumbling buzz descends on our family when Pam Young flies into town. I find myself casually dropping her name into conversations, "Pam? Oh, Pam is the author of *Sidetracked Home Executives: From Pigpen to Paradise*," or I will boast to my friends about Pam's appearances on the *Today Show*, *Live with Regis*, and *Oprah*. My children just laugh at me and simply share with their buddies, "Ila is coming to visit!" Pam, or "Ila" as the grandkids call her, is my dad's wife. In addition to being a creative author and a master conversationalist, she has a way of turning every task into a delight. During her annual two-week visit, our normally rushed dinnertimes morph into an enchanted story hour. Afternoon homework turns to deep conversations, and every evening closes with an original song or poem. In addition to bewitching my children, she happens to be a gourmet cook, while my Dad is a wicked efficient dish-washer. They are the ultimate houseguests and are welcome to visit me whenever they like.

As a stay-at-home mother of three in the 70s, Pam was a self-professed slob and wrote about becoming organized. Housework became manageable as she infused her mantra, "Make it fun and it will get done." This is now the heart of her website,* in which she encourages adults to find their inner child to gain control over habits, finance, weight, health, or organizational skills.

"Make it fun and it will get done" was the mantra I used to help my children get on board with my genuine food philosophy. This process had to be fun or it wasn't going to happen at all. Otherwise, I envisioned them packing their most sacred possessions into rolling suitcases and

* You can learn more about making it fun at www.makeitfunanditwillgetdone.com

heading down the cul-de-sac on a pilgrimage for freedom to eat what
they pleased. With my husband leading the way.

As meat portions diminished in our family and farm veggie choices
flourished, my most effective parenting tool was taste testing. We all
grabbed chunky crayons and rated foods using a color-coded system.
Purple meant the new veggie was fine. Red indicated it was tasty, while
green celebrated "more please!" (Notice the strategically missing option
for "yuck?") Flattered and excited to have their thoughts count, my children colored their way through farm stand food from May to October.

We had just as much fun with an assortment of organic popcorn and
local honey—ten varieties of kernels ranging from burnt umber, black,
and baby white; and mini honey jars collected from various locations,
both gifts from my brother. We sampled and compared the subtle differ-
ences in each honey and hypothesized whether the color of the popcorn
affected the flavor once popped.

As our family redefined what constituted a "treat," it became a treat
to let the kids choose one item at the farm stand without any conditions
from me. Evidently, freedom of choice goes a long way when you are
less than four feet tall, and my kids were more likely to enjoy the veggie
than if ol' Mom had picked it out for them.

We admired the farm-stand heirloom vegetables with their odd
shapes and variety of colors not found in the grocery store. Welcoming
their uniqueness, we modified names of some of the new-to-us-foods—
christening the dangling edamame peapods "who's-your-mommy
beans."

Occasionally I get to have some fun as well, and my idea of fun is a
road trip—to the extent that I wonder whether I may have descended
from Magellan. Or Sacajawea. Or possibly Dora the Explorer. A misty,
Sunday afternoon drive to the ocean or a three-day, multi-state adventure is all the excuse I need to open the sunroof, let my hand catch the
breeze from the open window, and listen to an entire John Denver CD.
The proof is reflected on my extra-freckled left forearm.

Our summer road trips used to be synonymous with fast food. From Wyoming to Washington, my family was always one game piece short of winning a Subway Scrabble or McDonald's Monopoly game. We found most meals spur-of-the-moment: convenient, cheap, and not a bit healthy. We would drive in and out to stay on schedule and arrive at our destination on time. Now, I was in quite a predicament with my newfangled thoughts on life. I had to change up our game plan and use online tools to create a list of potential green or organic restaurants for fresh, regional food en route. My own little "Food-ers" Travel Guide, if you will.

My family fell in love with flat bread pizza in Portland, Maine, topped with sundried tomatoes, locally grown baby spinach, and organic caramelized onions. Tentatively, we tried catfish on the outskirts of San Antonio, and it was a hands-down winner. The grass-fed hamburgers we enjoyed lakeside in Jackson Hole, Wyoming were unbelievable. Fabulous food is now part of our road trip destinations. The sense of exploration entices my kids to gladly abandon boxed meals served with toys. Now we shake our heads and chuckle, "What were we in such a hurry for in the first place?"

This is what I had to do. My kids had to experience involvement in order to appreciate genuine food. By infusing Pam's mantra "Make it fun and it will get done" into my attempt to change our family's eating habits, we shared the responsibility, and we grew together. My son and I constructed a compost bin out of chicken wire and stakes. We dabbled in vermiculture, which consisted of herding red worms in a Rubbermaid bin in the garage. (This part was more about togetherness than taste testing!) When winter settled in, we fondly reminisced about the taste of warm berries in our hand and the sweet pop of summer corn hot off the grill. And of course, we mocked my annual (failed) attempt at starting my own garden. Farm fresh foods were now images of summer to my kids—just as much as the neighbor's swimming pool.

Turns out, younger generations are empowered little humans. Born into the green revolution, they reduce, reuse, recycle, and celebrate with understanding. They embrace these ideas unabashedly. Somewhere deep in their DNA, far from marketers' reach, they, too, understand. One of my children talks of becoming a rancher; another, a baker; and another, an owner of a genuine food restaurant. Their dreams may shift, but I am sure one day when they leave their dorm room on a Saturday afternoon sporting tousled hair and flip-flops, they will peruse a local farmer's market to stock up on groceries, having a little fun along the way.

I couldn't be prouder.

Princess Pie,

So, Kaytee, to answer your question, "Am I organic?" I admit your question made me stop and think. I couldn't explain it to you just then because my answer wasn't easy, and it's not an easy time in our world. The last thing I want to do is make your life difficult. But your question reminded me of a wistful song Kermit the Frog used to sing when I was exactly your age. Sitting on a log alone, he would sing,

> It's not easy being green...
> Havin' to spend each day the color of the leaves.
> When I think it could be nicer being red or yellow
> or gold or something much more colorful like that.

Now I know, yes, yes I am organic. I am living, organic matter capable of life and decay. And so are you. For this reason, we should respect our body as if it is the most precious possession we own. Maintain it better than we maintain our cars. Nurture it more than we nurture our gardens. Listen to its signals more than we listen to our televisions. Our body and our one-acre are what we have. It's our responsibility to choose wiser when we can.

That is why I go out of my way to find food up to my standards to nourish your precious body. This may make me a food snob, but it turns out, I am proud to stand up for something I believe in. I hope you will be proud to stand up for the things you believe in too.

Now as you join me while shopping, I will try to be your role model. You watch me steer the cart straight to the organic produce and push right on by the rest. You may wonder why I have many questions for the butcher at the meat counter but rarely buy anything. Or why I choose to skip the cookies in order to splurge on a quart of organic strawberries for your lunchbox. When you are older, you will understand why I made these tough decisions. Because I love you.
Love,
Mom

.....and green can be like an ocean
or important like a mountain or tall like a tree.

When green is all there is to be,
it could make you wonder why, but why wonder,
Why wonder, I'm green. And it will do fine.

It's beautiful. And I think, it's what I want to be.

Immerse

Never doubt that a small group of thoughtful, committed citizens can change the world. Indeed, it is the only thing that ever has.

~Margaret Mead

Serendipity

My Choose Wiser workshops were growing and taking on a life of their own. There was an insatiable curiosity in the women at these events, and the buzz I felt being able to explain, show, and teach them motivated me to bring Choose Wiser to the next level. I established a website, started the Be Choosy newsletter, and began reaching out and posting tips on my newly created Facebook page. Supportive friends invited me to their circles. A book club here. A house party there. Then I used our family funds to reserve hotel conference rooms, created events, and invited my own guests. I felt a little like a child playing dress up, as I taught in meeting rooms with white linen tablecloths topped with complimentary bowls of mints and pitchers of ice water. My audiences ranged from small groups of three to wild and crazy groups of six women. Hardly enough to warrant a conference room, but I believed they were eager to learn and ready to push their standards of what would be acceptable in their own homes. They had coordinated babysitters, made an early dinner for their families, and slid on snow boots to brave winter weather to hear me speak.

For a while, I carried apprehension that hecklers would attend and challenge me. I wasn't quite ready for confrontational debate, but I was prepared to respectfully disagree and allow them to live by their own philosophies. During introductions, I braced myself when hearing that pediatric nurses and chemists had come to learn. Didn't they already know this information? Would they know more than I? By the middle of these workshops, I found they didn't form a peanut gallery as I had feared but were quick to vocalize support and provide stories from their profession that complemented my material. It was not unusual for audience members to be cancer survivors, caregivers of ill parents, or have a spouse undergoing chemotherapy. Just as disheartening to me were the moms who attended with focused hearts, trying to do everything possible to alleviate allergies, asthma, arthritis, skin disorders, and sensitivities—not for them necessarily, but for their children. Their resolve pulled at my heart, easing any trepidation I masked. Statistics I illustrated now had names; they were now daughters and sons. Understandably, many audience members came because they needed a night out or were coerced by friends or by me. (Heck, I'd be willing to listen to almost anything if it meant I could have an occasional night off from the child-bedtime rituals.)

Regardless of their stories, I warmly welcomed them, knowing they arrived hesitant and skeptical. As I began with a brief historical summary of how we got here, they listened with crossed arms, cocked heads, and furrowed brows. Thirty minutes later, a gratifying feeling bubbled inside me, as I witnessed their eyes light up, their body posture change to rapt attention, and the energy in the room begin to buzz. They were learning, and I was doing the teaching. They finally reached for the hotel-supplied note pads to scratch down thoughts and raised their hands wanting to ask more about the Skin Deep Database or endocrine disruptors. I introduced a new workshop on Genuine Food, after having made so much progress with my own family. I shared local food resources and an adorable video of my children and the Ladies. At the end of the evening, the women checked their watches, not believing how fast the time had gone by. They wanted to learn more yet were equally determined to go home and tackle a room or empty a purse to see what they could find. To share their experience with a coworker the next day. To search for a healthier meat or sign up for newsletters and email lists. When I returned home, I would retreat to my room with a spinning headache brought on by hours of concentration. All of this was worth every penny I handed over to the hotels. I was emotionally exhausted but deeply connected to a purpose.

All the months I spent researching, reading, and asking questions was now paying off—I was effecting change. Yet, the people I met through my workshops continued to inspire and change me as well. Catching up on my correspondences one day, I read an email from a participant I had met earlier that week. She wrote to encourage me to submit my story to a contest held by *Prevention Magazine*. They were holding a nationwide search for people who considered themselves "A Picture of Health." The email was sweet, but I wasn't a marathon runner.

I didn't climb mountains or try out for the Olympics. I did attend Yoga classes now and then, but this hardly classified me as an avid athlete or Picture of Health. Besides, I felt that entering a contest with that title while simultaneously trying to evade a recurrence of cancer would be the perfect way to jinx myself. I was about to thank her and delete the email, when I noticed an advertisement for *Prevention* in a stack of magazines at my feet. I wasn't a subscriber, and I hadn't received solicitation from them before. I smiled to myself and nodded. Okay, tell me more.

The contest defined the Picture of Health as one who had overcome a personal challenge, lived a healthy life, and inspired others. The entry deadline was the following week, and I would need to write an essay and submit a video clip. Figuring I had nothing to lose, I did both from my home and officially entered the contest. Three weeks later, on a Thursday evening during dinner dishes, I received a call from an editor at *Prevention Magazine*. I had been chosen. I was one of five people selected from across the nation out of close to a thousand entries. As part of this contest, the finalists would be featured in *Prevention Magazine* and appear on the national afternoon television show, *The Doctors*. True to American reality show culture, the winner would be chosen by email votes. I was instructed that if I chose to participate, I was not to tell a soul—BFF or local news agency. They would send the required legal documents swearing me to secrecy. Those who know me understand the restraint this took, as I'm not exactly a quiet, private person. In exchange for my silence and signature, I would be whisked off to New York City for a makeover and photo shoot. A little silence on my part for an opportunity to get my hair and makeup done by New York City professionals? It seemed like a no-brainer to me.

The morning of my trip, I wiped down the counter, emptied the garbage, fed the hens, and hopped a train to New York. Traveling by myself for four hours was a little slice of heaven—time I used to reflect on my circumstances. I had one shot at this. The only thing I needed to do was be kind. Be genuine. Enjoy this journey. I wondered if the four other contestants coming from across the country would be competitive. Were we supposed to be self-absorbed, creating a psychological mental edge? Was there an app I could download on five-minutes-of-fame etiquette? I suddenly lamented over never having watched *Real Housewives of New York City*. Surely, that show would have given me a few pointers on current New York attitude, clued me in on what to tip service staff, and alerted me to the posh vernacular du jour. At the very least, I would have known what martini to order.

I reached out to the contestants and suggested we meet for dinner and get to know each other. Due to travel logistics, only Linda was able to have dinner with me.

After a town car delivered me to my hotel, I headed to a neighboring rustic Italian restaurant. Braids of dried garlic hung from the plastered ochre walls, and the aroma from the smoky stone oven reminded me how hungry I was. It was fancy enough that three varieties of water were offered—tap, bottled, or bubbly—yet intimate enough that I could imagine resident celebrities feeling comfortable dining on a plate of gnocchi and chatting with friends. Linda arrived. Glowing. Her wide smile radiated a feeling of excitement and fun. Without pretension, we immediately started chattering. We were both simply delighted to be part of the contest. After we ordered, she asked the question we were both curious about. What was each other's story? No use acting shy. We might as well share—in six weeks, millions of subscribers would receive their magazines in the mail. Linda's story was truly amazing. The vibrant blonde across from me had formerly weighed three hundred pounds. Prepared for disbelief, she carried a manila envelope with dramatic "before" pictures of herself—a loving mom who had uncomfortably shied from the camera lens. Her large size had chipped away at her self-esteem for years. She initiated the change needed to lose one hundred and sixty pounds. Trim, sexy, and exuding passion, she shared her new life habits with support groups in her community.

In my eyes, our stories seemed very different. Breast cancer was plated and served to me; I had to deal and move forward. Linda's journey required extraordinary discipline and the initiative to start. With mutual respect established, she tried to understand what it was like for me to be a young mother faced with cancer, while I marveled at how healthy she appeared. I had assumed carrying excess weight would have made her heart, lungs, knees, and skin permanently cross with her, but her body was ecstatic to be free of the weight, and she glowed. How had she managed this incredible transformation? What habits did she break? What tools had she implemented? She had focused on small steps. On little changes. Her metamorphosis took time and faith. She shifted her meals and snacks from processed foods to simple, fresh fruits and vegetables. Meat portions diminished. Junk food disappeared. She utilized family support to make changes in her lifestyle.

Her journey was so different from mine yet strikingly similar. We had spent the last few years on parallel journeys. She was on a journey to lose weight, and I was focused on eco-health. Both of us incorporated real, fresh, simple food into our lives. Ultimately, we both used the intimate relationship between life and food to acquire healthy bodies. That's what all of this was about, wasn't it? That changing the way we ate and the products we used, left us with healthier, happier, bodies? The fact is that genuine food can give us this gift while processed food cannot. Meeting Linda was another "aha" moment for me. While she wasn't looking to cut out pesticides, fight cancer, or battle feedlots and big agribusiness, she became a healthier person by following similar ideals as I—two paths leading to the same destination. I loved this precious thought and tucked it away as my souvenir from my two whirlwind days in New York City.

The following afternoon, on my train ride back to yoga pants and motherhood, I reflected on the events of the past twenty-four hours. The entire day had been mind-blowing. I observed that clothing stylists, with rolling racks of high-end clothes, had the best job in the world. That playing dress up in four-inch heels and a periwinkle blue, Calvin Klein dress could make a girl feel sexy. That posing for pictures in front of a blowing fan was surreal. And that when a posh city hairstylist whips out scissors to cut the hair you've painstakingly spent months growing out, you smile and exclaim, "Absolutely! Cut what you will! These long locks were beginning to drag me down anyway!"

Exuberant, crazy madness followed. The contest issue hit the news-stands, and a nationwide email vote ensued. These votes, along with sponsor input, would determine the winner. That person would fly to Los Angeles, appear on *The Doctors*, and receive a $5,000.00 donation to a nonprofit of his or her choice. My goal was to hand the money to the Breast Cancer Fund and maybe take my kids to the San Diego Zoo.

Right Where I Am

"Ma'am, you need to throw that away. You can't go through security with that." The words from the cantankerous security woman jarred me from deep thought. It took me a moment to make the connection between her words and the strawberry-banana smoothie in my hand. Exasperated, I responded with a "chhh" and a "geez" under my breath. I heaved my laptop strap onto my shoulder, backed up my rolling suitcase, and squeezed between nosy, annoyed travelers. My emotions were bub-bling like a geyser, moving upwards toward my throat. I needed out fast. "Excuse me. Excuse me," I stammered, as I pushed through the crowd. Losing it was one thing. Losing it before trying to catch a flight was another, and I knew my frustration really wasn't about the strawberry-banana indulgence I was holding.

It was Tuesday afternoon. The voting period for *Prevention's* Picture of Health Contest had ended the previous Thursday after eight crazy weeks. I spent March repressing my excitement in silence, not able to divulge contest information with friends. April brought pandemonium as the issue hit newsstands, and America went online to vote for their favorite Picture of Health contestant. Since each supporter could vote once a day, the enthusiasm and rallying was continuous. I assumed it would only take a glance at the computerized tally and a meeting with sponsors to determine the winner. With the contest ending Thursday, I figured the winner would be notified by Friday. How hard could it be? It wasn't as if they were scrutinizing presidential hanging chads. Friday came and went without a yay or nay. Saturday and Sunday followed suit.

I imagined those in charge of the contest enjoying their weekend days by dining al fresco at a swanky New York bistro or tanning on their private beaches. Maybe the person in charge of announcing the winner was simply really bogged down with family laundry or grocery shopping and hadn't gotten around to divulging who had won. Whatever the reason, the silence was killing me. I jumped whenever the phone rang. While a part of me wanted to win, I wanted closure even more.

Mathematically, I had a twenty percent chance of being crowned the winner. The timing couldn't be better, as it was also my children's spring vacation. If we traveled, I secretly wanted to take them to see the baby panda at the San Diego Zoo. Yet, there was an eighty percent chance I would be writing a congratulatory email to the winner and exhaling with relief that the ride was over. Monday arrived with still no word, and my hope shifted to acceptance. One of the others must have won, and spring vacation was slipping away. My children tugged at me to replace plans of Hollywood tours with play dates at the park.

Thankfully, I had penciled in the Women's Health and Environment Conference in Pittsburgh, Pennsylvania on my calendar for this same week. I had intended to go but put it on the back burner waiting to see what would happen with the results from the contest. Now, the conference beckoned again. My compulsive (and a bit spiteful) psyche taunted, *You deserve it...come on ...what are you waiting around for? You didn't win, get over it,* and I booked the next morning's flight to attend the conference. (Granted, a bucket of organic banana ice cream and re-watching the 1980s movie *Working Girls* would have been a cheaper way to escape and deal with defeat. Hindsight is always 20/20.) My husband sensed it would be good for me to have space or (more honestly) better for him and the kids to have space from my tightly-wound self. Maybe my obsessive floor scrubbing and laundry folding gave it away. Or my snapping at the kids when they asked for, well, anything. He wholeheartedly supported my completely irrational, expensive departure. The next morning, I walked through Boston Logan Airport with long strides, energized with the tingle that comes from traveling alone.

I had the freedom to stay within my own thought bubbles, to choose the restaurant of my liking, to play Sudoku in pure silence. I didn't have to ration snacks for my hungry children or mitigate their bickering. This trip was all mine. I even considered having a drink on the flight. Surely, airlines served mimosas, right?

After I checked in at the airline counter, I treated myself to a mid-morning snack at the smoothie vendor. While I stood in line, I scanned my phone. And there it was. The announcement. An email from *Prevention's* editor-in-chief, Liz Vaccariello.

While in New York at our photo shoot, Liz had graciously dropped by to extend her congratulations to the contestants. You could feel the hushed respect from the ensemble of photographers and artists when she entered the studio. She was stunning, with dark, sleek hair and edgy bangs. An all-American, perky smile intertwined with New York executive polish. It was an honor to meet her, and it felt good to be acknowledged for my efforts to educate others about personal and environmental health. At that moment, I realized that one day, I too, wanted to celebrate other people who were making changes. I placed the thought onto my bucket list.

The closure I had been waiting for was now just a click away. In my head, I had pictured this moment differently. I had envisioned that I would be alone with my thoughts or surrounded by the comfort of my own home or even holding hands with my kids with eyes squinted shut. Thanks to my need to control my situation, I had booked a spontaneous flight, was surrounded by people I didn't know, and was waiting in line for a strawberry-banana smoothie. Not exactly the perfect time to get information of this magnitude—closure or not.

The email politely announced that the winner had been notified earlier that morning. Paula Bruchhaus, a spunky, spitfire, platinum blonde with a syrupy Louisiana drawl, whose weight loss inspired her community to live healthier lives, had been crowned the Picture of Health. *Well deserved.* I was truly happy for her. Then, like the morning after high school graduation, it was all over. The anticipation, the excitement, the anxiety ended just like that. Still standing in front of the food court, I slid out my boarding pass and license and headed to security.

This was where my mind was when the stone-cold security woman warned me liquids weren't allowed beyond that point. Like the twenty minutes it takes my brain to hear my stomach say, "All full down here, no more spaghetti," I reacted in slow motion to her request. The wheels on my suitcase caught on metal chair legs, as I tried to tug my way out of the line. I finally plunked myself down at a table to nurse my smoothie and gather myself. *Okay girlfriend. You have four minutes of pouting time. Repress it and you'll regret it. Acknowledge it so we can move on.*

I re-read Liz's email again. If I wasn't chosen, why had all this happened? What else was I supposed to learn? It felt so abrupt, and my life compass felt disoriented. A thought consoled me: it wasn't me, Kristi Marsh, who made the top five; it was the message of Home Eco-Momics and nontoxic living that was selected. It wasn't my makeover or flippy haircut that received thousands of votes; it was the environmental health message that resonated with many of *Prevention's* subscribers. An Everyday-Me had stood up for our right to health and earned a two-page spread during the process—in a magazine riddled with sponsors who might not have been crazy about my message. Sitting up a little straighter and nodding to no one, I thought, *I should be very proud. I've made progress. I've gained momentum.* And this journey wasn't over. I slurped the last of my smoothie, making sure to enjoy every delicious bit, and went in search of the bathroom to freshen up and get ready for my next unknown adventure.

Conventional Wisdom

The next morning, I eagerly arrived at the cavernous convention center decked out in heels and a dark purple business suit. Thousands of Everyday-Me's filed in carrying notepads, purses, and custom-made coffees, to listen to environmental scientists, writers, and activists, all sponsored by Teresa Heinz and the Heinz Endowments. Jumbo-tron-like screens hung from the ceiling to ensure the hundreds of tables in the room could see the lineup of speakers. To my absolute delight, Mia Davis, from the Campaign for Safe Cosmetics, texted me and invited me to sit in the empty seat next to her. Up front, center stage, second table back. It was like sitting at a white, linen-covered table in the front row of an *Oprah* taping. Sitting down in my chair, I felt my previous cravings to be ordinary come strikingly true. Compared to these women, I was a virtual nobody; I melted into a sea of role models, leading scientists, authors, and change-makers who chatted and laughed around me.

At that moment in time, I may not have been walking around the San Diego Zoo with my children, but I was in my very own version of Hollywood. Here, in this convention center, were real-time movers and shakers who had made dynamic contributions within the environmental health movement. Teresa Heinz, an international advocate for research for human health and wife of Senator John Kerry, sat at the table in front of me. Her book, *This Moment on Earth*, sat crisply on my desk at home, waiting to be read. To my right and left were the guest speakers for the day's event. John Peterson Myers, co-author of the groundbreaking book on endocrine disruptors titled, *Our Stolen Future*, was our host for the day. Bruce Lourie and Rick Smith, lanky Canadians and humorous writers, had people at their tables laughing. Their investigative book, *Slow Death by Rubber Duck*, followed their experiments of exposing themselves to everything from phthalates to mercury and then monitoring their own body burdens. During a stretch break, I shook hands and spoke briefly with Patricia Hunt, Ph.D., a modest and brilliant geneticist who worked at Washington State University. Ken Cook, founder of the Environmental Working Group, made us laugh and cry with his *10 Americans* story (already one of my go-to videos). And to top off my celebrity sundae with a cherry note of irony, at the end of the day, I introduced myself to Jeanne Rizzo of the Breast Cancer Fund, to whom I would have donated my winnings if I had won the *Prevention* contest.

With all the amazing talent that filled the room, Lisa P. Jackson, administrator for the EPA, left me star struck. WorkingMother.com had recently described her by saying, "Where environmental policy is concerned, Lisa Jackson is the most powerful mom in America." Yet, she humbly started her presentation by turning this around to the audience. "When it comes to the issues of toxic chemicals in the environment, in our bodies, our children's bodies, in our world, *you* are the most powerful women in America. It will be women, I promise you, who will change this debate forever." (Chills.) In her assured manner, she discussed the importance of modernization and reform of the Toxic Substances Control Act (TSCA). She became my hero. I was ecstatic to have this former chemical engineer in one of the most challenging positions in our government—our Environmental Protection Agency.

In her closing statements, Teresa Heinz followed with stoic emotion and a soft-spoken profoundness, "This is the first time I have ever heard an EPA Administrator say the things that were said today about the changes we are trying to force and instill and about the unavoidable consequences if we don't." At that moment, I knew I was witnessing living history. This wasn't research or learning to pronounce chemical names. This was evolution in the making. Like a little fly paralyzed on the wall, I didn't know where I was going, but I knew I was exactly where I was supposed to be. Immersed in the center of it all.

Immerse

1. to plunge into;
2. to involve deeply; absorb

Attending the conference rejuvenated my ambition, and I returned home ready to take on the last frontier—the place I immersed myself daily—my home environment. I had been shunning this space for months because the items to research and switch out were varied and encompassed many different departments and categories. Laundry detergent. Cleaning products. Toys and clothing. Plastic dishes and food storage containers. Indoor air quality. Dry cleaning. Furniture, carpet, and paint. Pet food. Pest control. As I mulled over starting points, it became clear these influential areas encompassed more than just my home; they spilled into the yards and schools where my kids spent most of their time. The list became immense and made this task unappealing to me. As soon as something starts to feel unmanageable, I put it off even longer. Like looking at laundry piled knee-high in every bedroom—the sheer amount of dirty clothes paralyzes me, and I'm reluctant to start, even if my kids don't have clean underwear. I needed to step back from the mounting list of household changes and remember what the goal was: to make the places where my family lived and breathed healthier. I couldn't change my children's schools (for now). I couldn't change all the yards they played in (except mine). Still, I could start by making changes to the inside of our home. I crossed many things off the list, and it began to feel possible. Again, I chanted my mantra, *One little change at a time, Kristi. Find what works, add it to the list, and move on.*

It was easy to procrastinate. I was much more attracted to creative items on my list, like working on my website or playing on Facebook. While I was consumed by developing Choose Wiser, my good friend Karen and her husband were well on their way toward changing out their four-step lawn care program for organic methods and creating homemade weed killer (a gallon of white vinegar, a bottle of lemon juice, and a ¼ cup of castile or dish soap). At the other end of our neighborhood, Tara had methodically evaluated cleaning products, replacing those with ammonia, chlorine bleach, and phosphates with kinder choices. She eliminated unhealthy cleaning products like a sharp-shooter at target practice, taking out the bad guys with rapid trigger pulls. With Tara and Karen running ahead of me on the same path, it was rather convenient for me to follow behind. Trusting their experiences involved less thinking and reminded me that the goal was a healthier home, not to recreate the wheel. Sharing our successes was a way to "work smarter, not harder," achieving the result with less overlap in effort. It was one thing to research what I did or didn't want in my dish detergent, but it was a blessing and time saver when my friends cut to the chase with tried and true experiences. "I tried making my own dish soap. No matter what, it left a film. I am happy with a store-bought eco-friendly version." Mulling over my to-do list, I realized I needed to employ a lot more girlfriends in my life.

To do this, I informally put the word out that I was looking for women who were interested in learning from each other. I'm a firm believer that we don't share our stories and strengths enough, and we spend too much time re-creating what someone is probably doing the next street over. Tapping into our invaluable female resources maximized learning and supported multi-tasking. I assured invitees they didn't have to be experts (none of us were), and we would focus on just a few subjects each time we gathered.

The first time the small, brave group assembled in Tara's basement family room, we kicked off with nail polish, sunscreen, and bug spray as our topics—areas we could speak of from personal experience to get the conversation rolling. Sure, nail polish and sunscreen were personal care products, but they were relevant for springtime and had healthier options. Books could tell us about recommendations, and EWG could share ratings, but in the real world, touch, smell, and application were just as important. Let's face it, how many times have we purchased or not purchased something because we didn't like how it felt or smelled, even if it was supposedly the "best"? By experimenting, we found some sunscreens applied like a thick layer of creamy toothpaste (not kid-friendly), while some water-based nail polishes would be great for little girls but didn't cut it for dishwashing hands. It was deeply satisfying to watch the interaction—our own modern-day quilting bee or barn raising—as we came together, passed down wisdom, and learned from each other. I resisted the formal feel of referring to it as a "club," so we affectionately referred to ourselves as the Gathering.

The second Gathering, inspired by the Women's Voices for the Earth Green Cleaning Party kit, has since become mini-legend. The Cleaning Party kit included recipe cards and labels for making homemade cleaning products. We started the evening in my living room, chitchatted around a table of appetizers, and tested organic wine. I facilitated the conversation and guided us through how we could replace chlorin-ated compounds, ammonia, and phosphates with simpler products. My favorite reference book, *Green Clean,* by Linda Mason Hunter & Mikki Halpin, highlighted the household cleaners we wanted to replace first due to their toxicity: carpet cleaners, drain cleaners, oven cleaners, and toilet cleaners. Our group was frustrated by the fact that cleaning prod-uct manufacturers did not have to fully disclose ingredients on their product labels. Maybe the list was too lengthy or might compromise precious trade secrets. Perhaps the companies thought we wouldn't care what was in our products; perhaps they felt we didn't have a right to know. We laughed at the irony in the adage, "They're sure housework won't kill you, but why take the risk?"

Before separating into stations around my home to mix and make products, I introduced my two new best friends: Ms. Baking Soda and Ms. Vinegar. These two rendezvous in various combinations in and out of my kitchen and around my home. Their strengths now took care of most of the dirty work. I hoisted the fifteen pound bulk bag of baking soda (about the size of a sack of potatoes and priced a little over three dollars) onto a table. Baking soda was multi-functional; it cut grease, scoured, deodorized, and mildly bleached. That's my kind of friend. While keeping baking soda as a household staple was relatively new to me, ladies chimed in with other baking soda tips: how to kill weeds in the brick walkway or scrub baked-on food from dinner dishes. Several women shared memories of their grandmothers using baking soda around the house, supporting my assertions that there was a time when cleaning products were a lot simpler and still effective.

Distilled white vinegar was the power cleaner and acted as a disin-fectant. This eased my conscience, as I constantly felt like I had to keep up with products that sanitize. Most people's rebuttal to vinegar is "but doesn't it smell?" While it does have a distinct smell, it deodorizes, and it dissipates quickly. For me, having to live briefly with the fragrance of Easter egg dye is an easy trade-off. Tara, who was previously affectionate toward the waft of chlorine bleach, said she grew to recognize vinegar as the new smell of clean.

It dawned on those of us at the Gathering, that we had spent a decade or two buying products of different sizes and colors, when all we needed were these two ingredients costing much, much, less. Personally, I felt duped for having been convinced that the only way to clean my home and the safest way to protect my children was to use the chemically laden products on store shelves. Now, I would mentally move that money over into the USDA Organic milk or happy hamburger budget.

Then we let the hands-on fun begin. To spice up the evening, I bought essential oils—lavender for its scent and tea tree for its disinfecting properties—to drop into our products. Each station consisted of measuring cups, a recipe card, masking tape, and a Sharpie. We filled previously-used salsa jars and butter tubs with ingredients for the recipes. To create a window cleaner, we measured water (squinting with our nearing-forty-something-eyes at tiny, measuring cup lines) and joked how we were convinced it was supposed to be bright blue to be effective. Silly us. At the stove, we ladled laundry detergent from a simmering pot into jars—after first verifying it would work in a front-loading machine without a problem. Olive oil and lemons waited for participants to make furniture polish, and I conveniently left rags nearby and encouraged them to try it on my dining room table. I admit I was disappointed when I prepared for the evening, as I hunted high and low for a spectacular, impressive recipe. But everything was simple. The most complicated concoction was a creamy, soft scrub that required mixing four ingredients.

We clinked, clanged, measured, and chatted about how crazy it was that we used cleaning products that had to be locked in cabinets or had warnings imploring us to use them in rooms with "adequate ventilation." Yet, how reassuring it was to make a furniture polish with ingredients found in pesto! Instead of sending the kids upstairs while I cleaned the bathroom, I could now invite them to measure, stir, and shake ingredients. Better yet, they could spray, scrub, and wipe as much as they wanted. Finally, we labeled and named our products with catchy phrases, such as "Mama's Window Martini" or "Pesto Polish-Hold the Cheese." We also wrote the recipe onto each container so it would be easy to make and replace when our supply ran low. We knew if we had to go searching out our recipe cards every time the product ran out, it would be one more obstacle in our path to success. Each of us was giddy and excited to take our products home to see if they really did the job. I offered to have everyone try them out by cleaning the bathrooms in my home, but sadly, there were no takers.

Robin Organ brought the whole point of the evening to the forefront. A slight, youthful brunette, she had the heart of a lioness—protective and fierce. She knew too well the interaction of environment and human health. She had nearly died from repeated anaphylaxis and toxic overload. Her body grew allergic to everything, including chemicals, food, and cleaning supplies. Robin's two daughters were suffering as well. To take back her family's health, she implemented simple strategies in their home, the next town over, and was now off medication.

With my friends captivated by her real-life story, Robin shared, "Each of us has an immune system, and our goal is to keep our immune system intact. If you think about your immune system as a bucket, you start to see symptoms when that bucket overflows. For someone like me, what fills my bucket could be yellow dyes, chemicals in the air, makeup, or toxic food. For someone who has diabetes, what fills up their immune system faster? We know sugars and other types of things would make that bucket overflow. The goal is to take those pieces out and let the immune system work so those symptoms literally disappear."

After rebuilding her body, she founded Greenschools, a nonprofit organization with the primary goal of empowering school environments. Children are immersed in classrooms, gyms, and cafeterias and can be exposed to cleaners, soaps, and disinfectants we are probably unfamiliar with. Greenschools offers many community services, including educating teachers, administrators, and school employees about green cleaning. They lead school assemblies with their band, using music to help children learn about sustainability. With her experience in the school systems, Robin encouraged us to get involved on any level. Once the children are excited, everything falls into place, and students start to initiate recycling, composting, or planning green fairs. "For the younger kids, this is the burden placed on them; they inherited all these problems, and they have to fix it. It has to start with kids." While Greenschools teaches younger kids how to pack a green lunch or middle school girls about cosmetics, my favorite tidbit is encouraging schools to seek alternative fundraisers and move away from selling junk food or wasteful wrapping paper and magazines. I need chocolate and paraffin candles like I need another synthetic-scented lotion. If we are trying to encourage our children to live healthy lives and make healthy choices, why do we ask them to sell products that don't support that?

Encouraging change in our schools takes time and patience, but it is possible. Robin shared, "When offering new ideas, strategies, and suggestions [to schools], it is best to come from a place of compassion and not one of judgment. Change in our schools can take longer than an individual parent may like to see, but schools need to care for hundreds and thousands of students and ensure they are doing right by all. I continue to be inspired on a daily basis by the hard work being done in our schools and am motivated myself to make a difference."

The Gathering, in whatever form—two friends, three sisters, or a Facebook community—is what we have while we push through. By comparing notes, we advance quicker. Standing around the kitchen island, we did what I had hoped for; we shared our ideas, successes, and attempts. We also brainstormed ideas for future Gatherings. How about learning the art of preserving food in August? Maybe vermiculture? Composting? Drying homegrown herbs? How could we encourage the preschools? The middle school girls? The high school teens? Maybe this would have been innate knowledge if we didn't live in such a transient society, but here among friends, we had each other. We created a network where ideas flowed. The best part of belonging to this group was that I was surrounded by like-minded women. Women who didn't think I was crazy for changing out my shampoos or buying organic produce. These women understood and agreed with my desire to immerse myself in the healthiest environment I was capable of creating. While many of my friends skeptically listened to me or shook their heads in disbelief at my stories, at the Gathering I no longer felt "out-there" for pursuing what I knew was right.

Future History

On a crooked, narrow street in the epicenter of Boston, a stone's throw from the Old South Church and Freedom Trail, Tanner, Kyle, Kaytee, and I entered the Massachusetts Department of Health. We passed through offices lined with metal file cabinets and decorated with putty-colored walls, flooring, and trim and arrived at our destination. About sixty metal chairs faced the front of the library-quiet conference room. I gave a friendly nod to fellow advocates I knew who would approach the microphone and speak about the proposed phase-out of the chemical Bisphenol-A (BPA) in our state of Massachusetts. There was no doubt the ban of BPA in reusable food and beverage containers used by children under three was needed. BPA is another one of those endocrine disruptors supposedly doing its job as a building block for plastics. Limiting the ban solely to wee-ones was not enough for me, and I was here to state my position. I ushered my kids to the back of the room. It was the first week of summer vacation. This wasn't exactly a day at the beach, but they sensed the seriousness of the moment and sat with church-like manners to witness policy-making in action.

Though I spent time every month at my local Toastmasters club to strengthen my public speaking, regretfully, I had passed notes in high school civics (many years ago) instead of learning the finer points of governmental processes. This information would have come in handy on days such as these, when I was to speak in front of a government advisory panel. Even though Elizabeth Saunders, from the Alliance for Healthy Tomorrow and Clean Water Action, warmly welcomed me and had encouraged me to testify, I was concerned I would mix my words, say House instead of Congress, or Sir instead of Your Honor. Would I have to face the small clique of polished professionals who were paid to be there to defend BPA in our economy? Would they throw tomatoes or write down my home address? I was worried I'd be outed as an amateur who didn't know what she was talking about. I closed my eyes and mentally pumped myself up. Yes, I was passionate about the subject, but still, testifying to the Department of Public Health was out of my comfort zone.

Due to my workshops and current-event reading, BPA's story was ingrained in my mind. Eighty years ago, it was created to be a synthetic estrogen, but the chemical DES (a more potent estrogen) was used instead. In the age of plastics, scientists found that BPA could be used as a building block in polycarbonate plastics. This meant no one could feign surprise when BPA started to interfere with hormone function. In fact, in 1998 Geneticist Patricia Hunt discovered that BPA leached from

plastic and corrupted her lab mice eggs as well as the following generation's eggs. We can find this highly unstable chemical in baby bottles, in
compact discs, in eyeglasses, in the lining of canned food, and in thermal
paper receipts. Very low doses of BPA—the levels we are exposed to
daily—are linked to a staggering number of health problems, including miscarriages, breast and prostate cancer, reproductive dysfunction,
metabolic dysfunction, behavioral disorders, and increased risk for car-
diovascular disease. [75] In 1970 the plastics industry created close to one
hundred million pounds of this compound and in 2004 they created
an unfathomable six billion pounds.[76] The Center for Disease Control
states that more than ninety-three percent of adults and children over
the age of six in the United States have measurable levels of BPA in their
urine.

The meeting commenced as two stoic men entered and sat at the
front of the room behind a folding table decorated with three micro-
phones and a quaint cassette tape player. I realized I would be presenting my points while sitting down, three feet from the panel, and with
my back to the audience. I wouldn't be able to use my tried and true
Toastmaster skills, the ones that made my other presentations stand out.
Interacting with my audience was not going to happen. An exuberant
smile would not help my case one bit. My mind scrambled, replayed my
presentation, and made adjustments. Because I brought my three children, they kindly bumped my presentation to the front of the line, so to
speak. I appreciate this sentiment when I'm standing in a long grocery
line with three complaining kids, but today I would have been happy
to speak last. Within my five minutes, I expressed my gratefulness to
businesses that provided alternatives to BPA (showing consumers BPA
wasn't necessary). I commended the Department for publicly advis-
ing that BPA might compromise chemotherapy (a little positive rein-
forcement goes a long way). I encouraged the two emotionless men in
front of me to allow our state to join the ranks of Minnesota, Vermont,
and Connecticut, by passing protective legislation; to be like Canada
and Norway who also took actions against BPA. Yes, I knew I could
stroll through my local Target and find reusable water bottles and baby

products proudly claiming to be BPA-free, as they should be. However, I explained I was an unusually aware consumer. Yes, legislation to protect children under three was critical, but what about toddlers and young children? What about protecting women of child-bearing age and their potential babies? This ban was only the first step. I shared the fact that I would continue to teach Massachusetts citizens, town-by-town, to use stainless steel water containers, to purchase fresh and frozen veggies instead of canned, to never use plastic in the microwave. I would continue to implore others to use glass containers to store leftovers, use foil instead of plastic wrap, and ceramic or glass cups and plates. My presentation traveled from passionate to angry and then to solemn.

I was painfully aware of the silence at the end. This is a killer to presenters everywhere, but evidently, in this public sector venue, no clapping was the norm. I returned to my seat and let my adrenalin run its course as another mom took the stand. I turned to my kids and asked if they were ready to tip-toe out of the room and proceed with our walk around Boston Common like I promised. All three of them shook their heads. They wanted to watch the meeting unravel. A slow, warm pride filled me.

The next woman at the microphone pleaded with anguish for our state to ban BPA—to protect other families from what she had endured. Her baby son had been born with hypospadias, a concern arising from fetal exposure to BPA and phthalates in consumer products during a small window of gestation. This condition alters the urinary tract of boys, requiring the babies to urinate out of a hole in the side of their penis and needing hours of reconstructive surgery. Data showed that hypospadias increased almost twenty percent between 1990 and 2000. Within minutes, tears welled in my eyes. I was humbled and felt helpless. What was *I* doing here? She had a real reason to fight.

Then, a man approached the table. He was a representative of a business association claiming the proposed ban would hurt businesses. I became agitated, emotionally charged. Furious, you could say. My mind silently retorted, *Innovative businesses—large and small—would adapt, not complain.* I understand that economic stability is a factor in many governmental decisions, but for too long it's been at the expense of our health. Was this man really concerned about the economy? Or concerned about selling his company's products that probably contain BPA? What he didn't seem to understand was people like me have stopped buying products with BPA, so he's already lost my business. His bottom line is already affected, just not in numbers that register quite yet. If enough people chose to boycott his products, his company would get the message that BPA was a chemical we didn't want leeching into our water or food. End of story. I'm always up for a good discussion or dialogue between opposing points of view, but listening to this man talk made my blood boil. In the interest of having a good day with my kids in the city, I decided to escort my wee-ones to the summer air where I could breathe.

Once outside, it was interesting that my children wanted to sit on a bench and people watch. Almost as if they needed time to reflect, as I did. We listened to the soft cooing of pigeons while I peeled an orange for our snack. I wondered if the pro-BPA testifiers would ever experience the heartbreak of their son being diagnosed with hypospadias and the subsequent surgeries. Would one of the two men on the panel be diagnosed with cancer? I wasn't inflicting voodoo, just thinking about statistics. With the probability of invasive cancers in men being one in two, I wasn't so far off. Would he spend his hours at Dana Farber Cancer Institute wondering if the BPA in his body interfered with the effectiveness of his chemotherapy?

Six months later, the Public Health Council unanimously voted to ban toxic BPA in baby bottles and cups, making Massachusetts the eighth state to do so. Certainly news to celebrate. However, this measure still leaves infants and toddlers vulnerable to exposure to the toxic BPA in infant formula cans and baby food packaging. It also didn't protect pregnant women's exposure to the chemical, which could have devastating effects on fetal development. [77] Being my first foray into government, I didn't know if this was a win or a loss. Should I feel angry that it wasn't a complete ban, or celebrate the movement forward? When it came right down to it, it was a change in the right direction. When our kids are little, we celebrate their first step. We clap and applaud them as they take the second and third, and eventually connect them together to run. Personally, I wanted to celebrate. It might be a while before these companies were running in the right direction, but I was willing to toast the movement forward.

Since that day, I've pushed aside the insecurities that prevented me from reaching out to my local, state, or national officials. Between you and me, I didn't think I would make a difference. Why would my representatives care what little ol' me had to say? I was just a carpooling-farm-stand-shopping-everyday-mom. Wouldn't those politicians employ active-listening body postures, turn on their political smile, and then kindly escort me right out the door? Becoming more involved in the political sector taught me that, yes, they did care very much about what I had to say. They may care for many different reasons, but the most important one is that I am a voter. A voter who does not keep quiet. A voter who talks to my neighbors, challenges the status quo, and strives to empower women to make changes through fun workshops. Who I was and what I had to say mattered. I learned I didn't have to memorize bill numbers or protocol; that was my congressperson's job.

I have always assumed politicians were bombarded daily with emails, phone calls, and people knocking on their door. All of the politicians on television dramas seem so busy! Isn't every person who works in Washington D.C. just oozing stress and busy-ness? (Except when they take an occasional time-out for an illicit affair?) However, squeaking wheels do get the grease, and discontented rumblings do attract your representative's attention. Their scanners are always on—monitoring what growing sentiments are pulsing in their districts. They also talk amongst each other just as we do. (Except they are in expensive suits and heels.) They meet over coffee, have lunch, and chat at events, sharing and exchanging information. *"Barney, how are you doing? Can I get you a coffee? Hey, listen, have you heard about the toxins in personal care products? My constituents are very passionate, and you are a co-sponsor on the bill....fill me in..."* Matter of fact, until I went knocking

176

one afternoon, my congressperson's office wasn't even aware of the legislation I was addressing! After I left, they knew more about it. They knew I was interested in it and willing to stand up for it. If we bring something to their attention, they will seek more information. We have to push upward and share how we feel. I am convinced things will change. It is just up to us to decide when. Now? In ten years? Will it be another generation's efforts? From now on, I will never miss an opportunity to make my voice heard.

The Proclamation

I love when my kids get on the bus in the morning. The house is quiet, and I begin my morning ritual—grab my oversized mug of hot tea, fold my legs beneath me on my swivel chair, and surf current events online. During one such ritual, I came across an article in the *New York Times* written by Nicholas Kristof. [78]

> "The President's Cancer Panel is the Mount Everest of the medical mainstream, so it is astonishing to learn that it is poised to join ranks with the organic food movement and declare: chemicals threaten our bodies."

> *This panel is like Mt. Everest? This must be big.* I ventured further.

> "The cancer panel is releasing a landmark two hundred page report on Thursday, warning that our lackadaisical approach to regulation may have far-reaching consequences for our health. It calls on America to rethink the way we confront cancer, including much more rigorous regulation of chemicals."

Wow. *What's going on here?* My mind raced like fingers running through an old library card system. P..P..Pres..President's Cancer Panel...what was that? The closest thing my mind could recall was the elementary school Presidential Physical Fitness Test. The one where I mortifyingly failed the timed pull-ups test in fifth grade. (I had tiny biceps back then.) This clearly wasn't the same thing.

A little more snooping brought me up to speed. The President's Cancer Panel was created in 1971; its job is to report recommendations to the President and guide the priorities of our National Cancer Program. Appointed by former President George W. Bush, the current panel was preparing to report to President Obama. The panel had convened over two years to gather testimony on the state of environmental cancer research, policy, and programs and was now poised to publicly acknowledge that many known or suspected carcinogens were completely unregulated. The report was not singular to cancer but acknowledged environmental toxins were factors woven into learning disabilities, neurological issues, reproductive disorders, and hormone disrupting chemicals.

The letter from the panel advised the President to "use the power of your office to remove the carcinogens and other toxins from our food, water, and air that needlessly increase health care costs, cripple our nation's productivity, and devastate American lives." Some of the information gathered and formalized in the report was not breaking news but as old as the prolific usage of synthetic chemicals themselves. For decades, survivors, fighters, researchers, scientists, and Everyday-Me's had been working and supporting this movement. This was the first time in forty years the Cancer Panel recognized and publicly declared the link between environmental causes and triggers of cancer. This proclamation seemed to ordain existing links and science as official.

I was cautious before posting on my Choose Wiser Facebook page or drafting a Be Choosy newsletter. I watched. I waited for the "other side" (anti-health lovers? synthetic chemical lobbyists?) to roll out a hired expert scientist to shoot down the message, to illuminate the loopholes and failings in the report. I waited. I did laundry, returned, and refreshed the computer screen. Nothing. I washed some dishes and fed the chickens, returned, and refreshed my computer screen again. Still nothing. The naysayers never came. In our normally bickering world, it left the oddest sense of silence. A stillness encompassed a rare sense of togetherness, a feeling of the vast possibilities that lie ahead. Or maybe it was just the warm cup of tea in my hand and the peacefulness of a house without children that had me feeling so nostalgic. Whatever the reason, I was stunned that no one had come forward to start a negative dialogue.

The article also went on to explain that the report specifically stated, "raising consumer awareness of the risks is imperative." *Hey! Wait! That's me!* IMPERATIVE. Oh, what a lovely, handsome, strong word! I turned this statement into an adventure. There was a glimmer of hope, as I interpreted the prestigious panel's words as: *People of America! Educate yourselves on the unregulated, environmental toxins in your surroundings! Go forth and learn! Your awareness is vital, your participation is required. It is* Imperative.

A few months later, I listened to one of the panel members, Dr. Margaret L. Kripke, speak at Harvard University. She explained that the role of the panel was to advise, which it did. That was as far as its powers extended. The panel did not create laws. It could not make the President act or react in one manner or another. Bewilderment crossed many of the faces in the audience, including mine. Why wasn't this panel more powerful? Why spend all the time reporting findings if it was unable to do anything about them? Would this important information be filed away in the minutes of a meeting, never to be heard from again? After some thought, I realized the government was not our rival or a place to point fingers and place blame. *We* are the government. Even without an official title, we must use our voices. We have the nonprofit organizations in place. We have local governments listening. We have the historical declarations of the President's Cancer Panel report.

The world is shifting, preparing for change. At the beginning of this journey, I had to focus on my home and my one-acre in order for me to absorb the immensity of the subjects I was learning about. Focusing on these areas made the tasks manageable. I felt good about the new products we were purchasing, the foods we were eating, and the items I used in and around my home. Now that I was stronger and more aware,

I realized I could slowly allow my passionate views to influence other surroundings. I could go beyond my one-acre. I could start looking at how to encourage change in my children's schools. Instead of feeling insignificant, I realized I had the power to educate and encourage our government to support legislation that would protect our inalienable right to health. My life hasn't turned out the way I had envisioned when I was a girl swimming in Clear Lake—it has become something more beautiful than I imagined possible. I have a purpose and a mission that fuel and energize me, even on days I feel overwhelmed. I set out on this journey intent on building a new body, but what I built was a new me. I wanted to initiate healthy changes in my family and realized that in the process, I could show other women it didn't have to be difficult. It didn't have to be expensive. It was possible to choose wiser, select simpler, and respect the body.

You, too, are worth it.

The opening letter of the President's Cancer Report, April 2010.

Dear Mr. President:

Though overall cancer incidence and mortality have continued to decline in recent years, the disease continues to devastate the lives of far too many Americans. In 2009 alone, approximately 1.5 million American men, women, and children were diagnosed with cancer, and 562,000 died from the disease. With the growing body of evidence linking environmental exposures to cancer, the public is becoming increasingly aware of the unacceptable burden of cancer resulting from environmental and occupational exposures that could have been prevented through appropriate national action. The Administration's commitment to the cancer community and recent focus on critically needed reform of the Toxic Substances Control Act is praiseworthy. However, our Nation still has much work ahead to identify the many existing but unrecognized environmental carcinogens and eliminate those that are known from our workplaces, schools, and homes.

To jump-start this national effort, the President's Cancer Panel (the Panel) dedicated its 2008–2009 activities to examining the impact of environmental factors on cancer risk. The Panel considered industrial, occupational, and agricultural exposures as well as exposures related to medical practice, military activities, modern lifestyles, and natural sources. In addition, key regulatory, political, industrial, and cultural barriers to understanding and reducing environmental and occupational carcinogenic exposures were identified. The attached report presents the Panel's recommendations to mitigate or eliminate these barriers.

The Panel was particularly concerned to find that the true burden of environmentally induced cancer has been grossly underestimated. With nearly 80,000 chemicals on the market in the United States, many of which are used by millions of Americans in their daily lives and are un- or understudied and largely unregulated, exposure to potential environmental carcinogens is widespread. One such ubiquitous chemical, bisphenol A (BPA), is still found in many consumer products and remains unregulated in the United States, despite the growing link between BPA and several diseases, including various cancers.

While BPA has received considerable media coverage, the public remains unaware of many common environmental carcinogens such as naturally occurring radon and manufacturing and combustion by-products such as formaldehyde and benzene. Most also are unaware that children are far more vulnerable to environmental toxins and radiation than adults. Efforts to inform the public of such harmful exposures and how to prevent them must be increased. All levels of government, from federal to local, must work to protect every American from needless disease through rigorous regulation of environmental pollutants.

Environmental exposures that increase the national cancer burden do not represent a new front in the ongoing war on cancer. However, the grievous harm from this group of carcinogens has not been addressed adequately by the National Cancer Program. The American people— even before they are born—are bombarded continually with myriad combinations of these dangerous exposures. The Panel urges you most strongly to use the power of your office to remove the carcinogens and other toxins from our food, water, and air that needlessly increase health care costs, cripple our Nation's productivity, and devastate American lives.

Sincerely,
LaSalle D. Leffall, Jr., M.D., F.A.C.S. Chair
Margaret L. Kripke, Ph.D

Pioneer Girls

Butterflies all havin' fun you know what I mean
Sleep in peace when the day is done, that's what I mean
And this old world is a new world
And a bold world
For me....

~ written by Anthony Newley and Leslie Bricusse

Circling the Wagons

f you married a man from Casper and visited his parents over summer vacations, you might find yourself on various day trips, cruising
along the high plains of central Wyoming. With your feet up on the
passenger dashboard, you might think the dry, burnt umber layers
in the craggy outcrops are an entertaining diversion from the miles and
miles of plateaus, which look pretty much the same, give or take an
antelope or prairie dog. After passing the town of Muddy Gap and far
from anything else, you would approach Independence Rock, probably
relieved for the opportunity to stretch. You might slide on flip-flops.
Maybe toss your unfoldable map onto the floor and announce, "All right
kiddos, power off, everyone out." That's if you married a man from
Wyoming. Which is what I did and where I found myself the summer
after my cancer treatments ended.

For us, Independence Rock was our destination—our attempt
to expose our children to some tangible American history and culture. Watching the film *Dances with Wolves* is one thing, but actually
breathing the Wyoming air is another. When we arrived, Ted herded
the kids toward a restroom. Hot air filled my lungs, as I stepped
from the air-conditioned minivan into the sauna-like surroundings.
I adjusted my bunched shorts and tightened my ponytail, pleased
I finally had a ponytail to tighten. With a few blessed minutes to
myself, I twisted right and left, swung my arms, and loosened my
traveling joints. I slid my clunky, Canon Rebel camera over my neck
and placed the strap of our soft-sided cooler—containing crackers,
cheese, grapes, and water—over my shoulder. As I gathered our
things, an intensely purple flower caught my eye. Bristly like a paint-
brush, the size of an engorged strawberry, it reached confidently
toward the sun away from its broad, dusty-green leaves. Maybe it
was a mild case of heat stroke, but I sensed this flower wanted me
to take her picture. (I suppose the flower could've been male; for
me, flowers are female although I did resist the urge to name her.)

I adjusted my lens to zoom and added the image of this thistle to my collection to be uploaded when I returned home. Nearby were also mounds of thigh-high, twiggy, sagebrushes. I reached over, rubbed the thin, grey-green leaves between my fingers, and savored its earthy scent. The sparse vegetation surrounding me consisted mostly of sagebrush and a smattering of the flowering thistle. Both plant species had evolved within the extremes of bitter winters and hot, dry summers. Quite the little survivors.

During the years before Rachel Carson wrote *Silent Spring*, our nation copiously sprayed millions of acres with chemicals, in hopes of turning the sagebrush country into lush, cattle grasslands. Carson pointed out that applying synthetic chemicals didn't just destroy the sage but the life it nurtured and that coexisted with it. The chicken-sized grouse nested beneath its spindly branches; the antelope, deer, and moose grazed on the indigenous plant life; the willows further west were unintended recipients of the caustic chemicals, which then affected the beavers that fed on them. When the beavers ceased building dams, the lake drained away and the trout had no habitat. Carson wrote, "None could live in the tiny creek that remained, threading its way through a bare, hot land where no shade remained."[79] All of this devastation was a result of our desire to grow grasslands for cattle.

Standing in that relatively desolate area, I closed my eyes and welcomed the hot wind. Its movement eased the intensity of the hundred-degree heat. Depending on the time of year, the wind might be warm and refreshing or nasty and bitter, but it seemed to me it was always, always, blowing. While most of the local craggy landforms earned names like "Devil's Gate" and "Split Rock," the constant wind had sculpted Independence Rock into an enormous slumbering whale, approximately twenty acres in size and several stories high. Polished and rounded by wind and weather, it was a beautiful example of nature's tireless, artisan hand.

While the kids hunted for devious, elusive prairie dogs, I learned more about the legend of Independence Rock. Like many of central Wyoming's tourist destinations, the story unfolded around the early 1800s when over five hundred thousand immigrants and pioneers traversed the Oregon, Mormon, and Californian trails. They traveled these trails leaving thirty-nine thousand marked and unmarked graves along the way. They often started their pilgrimage at the Missouri River in spring, moved across these very plains, and then climbed, maneuvered, and ascended the mountain ranges, covering nearly two thousand miles. They walked. Or pushed handcarts. Or used oxen to pull canvas-covered wagons. Regardless of how they arrived, it was critical to hit this very spot by July. Timing was crucial to survival if they wanted to successfully pass through the Cascade Mountain Range or the Sierra Nevada before the throes of winter descended.

As waves of Mormons, traders, trappers, and emigrants passed through this area, they used tools, tar, or buffalo grease to engrave or mark their names and dates onto Independence Rock, leaving a visual legacy of those who had passed here centuries earlier. This was a way to communicate to fellow friends and family that at least up until this point in their journey, they had made it safely. Yes, cell phones would have been much easier, but that wouldn't have left quite the visual history like a hand-carved name in stone. Successive travelers would stop to make camp and scrutinize the rock for signs of a sister, a son, or a longed-for husband. In the early 1850s, Lydia Allen Rudd wrote in her journal, "Came to independence rock about ten o'clock this morning [sic] I presume there are a million of names wrote on this rock…saw my husband's name that he put on in 1849." These messages were a far cry from the instant texting updates I carried on with my husband. How good it must have felt for Lydia to get to this point on her journey and see her husband's name! How hopeful those early travelers must have been when they reached this notorious spot.

In solemn observance, my eyes ran over the names and marks blasted by decades of dust and wind. Legible dates, moments of American history frozen in time, echoed within me. I had a deep respect for these unnamed, everyday settlers who pushed their families to unfathomable limits in search of better opportunities. I understood their willingness to leave everything behind in search of a sanctuary to call their own. Whether they fled for freedom of beliefs or pursuit of riches, ultimately, they sought a better life. In my mind, I envisioned my own Independence Rock, chiseled with the names of people whose intense passions have helped shape this country in a different way, preparing an environmental health path for followers. Rachel Carson's name is deeply engraved here, along with fresher signatures from authors Stacy Malkan and Michael Pollan. What gave pioneers such resolve to blindly push into the unknown? Was it the human spirit, not the pioneers themselves, that protected and took risks? Took poison in order to heal? Endured in order to embrace? If it's the human spirit, and not simply a factor of existing within a certain era, then we are all capable of change. It is still possible to push ourselves from the comfortable resting place of status quo and onto a path where we question our choices, demand safer products, and choose wiser for our families.

Sure, I profess to select simpler, but my constant references to a journey could hardly be compared to what these people endured two hundred years ago. I stood in my flip-flops, cell phone in my back pocket, having the knowledge that in three hours we would enjoy a barbeque dinner on Grandma Hope's patio, followed by splashing in the hotel pool before going to bed. It might be exhausting, but it was hardly a tribulation. We wandered Independence Rock for another hour and soaked up the history it represented before heading back to our minivan. While I was awed by the thought of the thousands who walked through this very place, a thankful spirit danced inside me. I was grateful, relieved, and a tad self-righteous that I didn't have to leave everything behind and endure a two-thousand mile pilgrimage into the unknown.

Occasionally, after a Choose Wiser workshop, an audience member will stare at me the same way I stared at that rock, trying to imagine what my cancer-patient life was like, what she would have done if she had gone through the same trials. Shudders of *I'm-so-glad-I'm-not-dealing-with-that* race through her mind and down her spine. Her eyes reflect a mixture of awe and pity. I recognize it instantly, only because I used to view others in the same manner. Amidst an after-presentation-buzz, she might approach me with, "I was really amazed by your presentation. Everything you went through and all, I mean with the cancer. You really do a lot to stay healthy. Good for you. I don't know if I could ever do all that."

And there it is. The misunderstanding. Regardless of how many times I hear it, it still unsettles me. My confidence shrinks, and I squirm and stutter. My smile freezes awkwardly in place, and my mind races. My presentations weren't about being a cancer patient. They weren't really about me. Running my fingers across a tumor in the shower just happened to be my personal detour. The process of our lungs inhaling and exhaling, the profuse manufacturing of red and white blood cells, or hair growth observations isn't unique to those recovering from disease. Everyone's bodies do these things every day. Every minute. This wasn't about cancer, diseases, or disorders. This wasn't about revenge, anger, or revolt. This was about health. My health. My children's health. Your health. Our collective human health. My pioneer journey is about respecting the body and embracing life.

But I don't say it. Instead, I thank her, shake her hand, or give her a hug. I don't explain or provide an entire coursework on environmental health. I understand that learning is a process and a journey for everyone, and we are all at different points on our trip. I chalk it up to, "It's just not her time." I trust her day will come. There was a reason she was at my presentation, a reason I will never know. The goal of my message is to plant a seed and believe it will grow and unfold when the time is right.

After Independence Rock, we made one more stop in the day's travels. In my children's eyes, it was more of the same: heat and dirt. They begged to go back to Grandma's house, but like all good mothers intent on making a learning experience out of vacation moments, I tried to force appreciation on them by pointing out, "Hardly anyone you know will ever get the chance to be here!" Mainly because we were in the middle of absolutely nowhere. "See what you get to see! You are so lucky!" I directed them toward the wagon wheel ruts that ran parallel to the road, carved into the crust of the earth almost two centuries old. This was just as exciting as watching the latest movie or playing the newest version of Super Mario Brothers, wasn't it? Well, I knew it wasn't. But parenting is all about how we spin it.

My mind's image of a pioneer is a singular renegade; a solitary revolutionary. Lonely. Viewing these deeply rutted wagon trails clarified that the destination was reached in tremendous numbers. At the end of the day, it took more than one wagon to create a circle. Within these migrant communities, they shared resources, educated each other, and took care of one another in illness. They shared the grief of losing husbands or children and encouraged each other to continue on. There is something incredibly moving to me about locking arms and coming to the side of another. In togetherness, we find safety and strength. Standing together, we become pioneers.

Making changes in my home alone does not make me a forerunner in the environmental health movement. Many other people have gone before me and have established organizations that help to further this cause. The Campaign for Safe Cosmetics, Women's Voices for the Earth, Breast Cancer Fund, Collaborative for Health and the Environment, Healthy Child Healthy World, Organic Consumer Association, Certified Humane®, and countless other nonprofits have sent armies of Everyday-Me's ahead. Each organization had a starting point. Before those people rallied or educated others, they were once children. Before our protection became a science, a website, or a law, it stemmed from a thought, a gut feeling, an instinct to protect our one-acre.

Our journey is not physically traipsing two thousand miles but in shifting our routines and thought. It might be just as difficult but in different ways. We aren't fighting Asiatic cholera or protecting our children from an angry buffalo, but we are constantly battling against television commercials, pretty packaging, and convoluted marketing. We are always fighting for more time in our day as we juggle careers, soccer practice, karate, and scouts. We compare ourselves to other women and mothers who seem to be doing things better than we are. Regardless of how much effort we put into trying to do the "right thing," we sometimes feel it isn't enough.

Choosing wiser isn't about guilt. (Or cancer.) It's about moving toward a healthier lifestyle by influencing what we smother on our skin, the foods we devour, and the surroundings in which we immerse ourselves. It's about encouraging innovative businesses and diligently supporting active change to protect the generations ahead. Then we too can take a pocketknife (or buffalo grease) and scratch our names into the rock, declaring we were here. We cared. We made a difference. We are pioneer girls, one little change at a time.

Dear Reader,

The last few years have produced many changes for my family, yet from the outside, it would appear much is still the same. I love food and probably snack too often when passing through the kitchen. I still wear makeup and use raspberry lip stain. I begrudgingly clean my home. I go to sleep questioning if I'm doing the right thing or if I spent enough time with my kids that day, always searching for balance. My children still struggle to understand the world of intense marketing and will probably always want to order soda when we dine out. I will always grimace and struggle within. They are more aware as children than I was for most of my adult life. I am preparing them to challenge the status quo; I am helping to shape the parents they will become. Really, this book is for them: the children who will become our scientists, politicians, business leaders, doctors, engineers, and farmers. They are always watching and learning from us; if it is important to us today, it will be important to them tomorrow.

The key is just to start. Take one product or room or food item, and make a wiser choice. Replace it, and move onto something else. Pour yourself a margarita, and dance around your newly purchased farm stand spinach. Celebrate your new deodorant, the tomatoes you grow, or the cleaners you made, instead of focusing on what you still have left to do. I've been changing things around my house for four years now, and there are still many items on my list. View change as a process and not as a destination, and tasks become adventures. There is no end to this journey. It is a life-long philosophy to embrace, not a singular lesson to check off. I have found (sigh of relief), that once change is part of the routine, it becomes easier to continue.

A picture comes to my mind that best conveys my intended purpose: one of me straddling a three-rail fence that separates the rolling, hilled pastures from the daily commotion. I balance there in the sun, in my faded jeans, boots and cowgirl hat, smiling and reaching down to give a friendly hoist to those arriving from the busy, hurried world. Once on the other side, caring, curious, Everyday-Me's learn, play, and embrace the idea of being an advocate for their own beautiful bodies. That's my place. A fence straddler.

To accomplish that through the written word, I intentionally exposed my emotions to illustrate how we are more alike than we are different. I don't view myself as a green goddess or an eco-diva; instead I mock my insecurities and reveal my anger. I might have even let my sarcastic side slip once or twice. My story is not all encompassing; it does not touch on many other important issues such as seafood, environmental justice, or current legislation. I did not set out to write a book on cancer statistics; there are plenty of authors who have done that. I did not set out to write a story solely about my breast cancer experience, as there are many women with stories much more compelling than mine. Instead, I offered an appetizer plate of information, allowing you to test, try, and nibble before deciding upon your meal. I set out to inspire you through a real woman with an honest voice. I invited you to witness my personal grief and shared stories I hadn't revealed to my family or closest friends. The words tapped into my keyboard poured from my core and out my fingertips with the desire to cause discussion.

   Little Changes encompasses an enormously weighty message, difficult to explain to others in a spiffy, thirty-second clip. You don't have to be an expert to share—just a caring human. Let your friends and family have the opportunity to decide for themselves by gifting, sharing, or recommending this book. I wrote this because my journey started with a lump and a diagnosis and maybe, just maybe, someone else's journey can start with this book.

Enjoy the journey.

Kristi Marsh

Thoughts from Stacy Malkan

"We are the ones we've been waiting for."

June Jordan, poet

I am honored Kristi asked me to write this afterword. Hearing about her story—from her devastating cancer diagnosis to her remarkable journey to her triumph of finding her own strong voice and purpose in the world—inspires me more than I can say. If one person can have such an impact, imagine what we could do if everyone started making little changes!

I've been fortunate in my own work to have a close-up view of what's possible when we work together. When a small group of women founded the Campaign for Safe Cosmetics in 2002, we had no idea how far we could take our efforts to shift the beauty industry away from toxic chemicals. Nearly ten years later, our nonprofit coalition has instigated major changes in this $50 billion dollar industry.

In 2006, we celebrated the news that every major nail polish manufacturer agreed to stop using the "toxic trio" of chemicals: toluene, formaldehyde, and dibutyl phthalate. The victory came after a two-year effort that involved thousands of letters and media stories pointing out the double standard that companies were already making safer nail polish in Europe where the laws are stronger.

Most recently, working in collaboration with health groups such as the American Nurses Association and Physicians for Social Responsibility, we were able to convince Johnson & Johnson to reformulate hundreds of baby products around the world to remove cancer-causing chemicals.

The Campaign for Safe Cosmetics first reported in 2009 that "pure and gentle" Johnson's Baby Shampoo contained two carcinogens—formaldehyde and 1,4 dioxane—that were not listed on the label. Over the next two and a half years, the campaign and our allies sent letters and met with Johnson & Johnson executives many times to raise these concerns. While the company launched a new "natural" carcinogen-free baby shampoo (at twice the price of the original), they made no move to change the formula of the iconic bright yellow shampoo.

In the fall of 2011, the campaign released a second report comparing the American version of Johnson's Baby Shampoo to the same shampoo sold in a dozen other countries. We were not surprised to find the company was already making safer formaldehyde-free shampoo in countries such as Sweden and Japan, while continuing to use formaldehyde chemicals in products sold here in the United States.

This type of double standard doesn't sit so well with parents, and within hours of obtaining our report, Johnson & Johnson made a public commitment to reformulate all their baby products worldwide to remove quaternium-15, a formaldehyde-releasing preservative, and reduce 1,4 dioxane to the lowest possible levels. They also announced that they had already removed phthalates from the fragrance in all their baby products. This is a major victory for babies and a big step in the right direction!

While we wait for big companies to make big changes, there are currently safer products out there we can use. Over 321 companies already fulfill all the promises of the Compact for Safe Cosmetics, a pledge to make safer products. You can find out more about these Champion companies at www.SafeCosmetics.org/MarketShift.

Every positive step we take is getting us closer to a future in which all products on all shelves are safe for all people. Companies are listening to consumer's demands for safer products and the industry is changing.

The big changes are made up of thousands of little changes that you are making every day.

Kristi wrote, "as long as I'm moving forward, I'm headed in the right direction. I like to think there was a time of uncomplicated products—when families ate simple, unprocessed foods, used straightforward cleaning ingredients—and there will be a time in the future. Our current lives happen to exist in a time of change."

That's exactly right and I think it's an exciting time to be alive. We have the choice right now and every day to embrace change, and together, to create the world we want to live in. Here's to the little changes beginning, continuing, and growing!

Stacy Malkan
Co-founder, Campaign for Safe Cosmetics
Author of *Not Just a Pretty Face: The Ugly Side of the Beauty Industry*
www.SafeCosmetics.org
www.NotJustaPrettyFace.org

Forty Little Changes

Straightforward & budget-friendly actions to respect the body.

SMOTHER

- ☐ Choose nail polish free of formaldehyde, toluene, and dibutyl phthalate. Or let your nails tap around nude.
- ☐ Bring your own polish and hand lotion to salons.
- ☐ Use less of everything. Instead of dollops, use squirts.
- ☐ Check toothpaste, antibacterial soaps, and personal care products for triclosan. Surround yourself with products that don't have it.
- ☐ You smell wonderful. Skip colognes and perfumes. Or use ones created from essential oils.
- ☐ Lice. Eww. Suffocate the buggars with olive oil and a plastic shower cap, and skip the insecticide treatment.
- ☐ Fill a squirt bottle with diluted cider vinegar and place in the shower. Rinse through hair after shampoo and conditioner for soft, luxurious locks.
- ☐ Gray is simply classy. Hair coloring ingredients? Not so pretty.
- ☐ Refuse to give up your dye job? Choose a color closer to your natural for fewer applications. Choose an ammonia-free product line. Or talk to your stylist about foiling in henna with paper wraps.

DEVOUR

- ☐ Plant a patio herb garden.
- ☐ Choose fresh food over frozen, frozen over canned.

- ☐ Buy seasonal, organic, local food in bulk.
- ☐ Intimidated by canning? Freeze! Keep a container for all sorts of leftover fruits. Use in the winter for smoothies or toppings. Keep another container for veggies for soups.
- ☐ The fattier the meat, the more potential dioxins and chemicals that could be stored in it. Choose, cook, and eat less.
- ☐ Give fruits and veggies a cold shower in the sink. Scrub the firm, soak the leafy.
- ☐ Kiss your food. Then masticate slowly. Appreciate and savor instead of inhale.
- ☐ Plastics. If you have to have them, check the recycle code and chant: *#7, #6 and #3 are not for me.*
- ☐ Artificial colors are so 1980s! Give your food a makeover, and be done with yellow 6, blue 1 and 2, green 3, and red 3.
- ☐ Use reusable aluminum or BPA free containers for filtered water. Fill 'em up after each washing, and line 'em up in the fridge side door for easy access.
- ☐ Have some happy meat to barbeque? Take it easy on the flames, and go for the un-charred look.
- ☐ Pop popcorn kernels in a pot with some oil. Bag the microwave bag.

IMMERSE

- ☐ Dust. Use a microfiber cloth to dust. Much easier when done to the *Grease* Soundtrack. Less stuff = fewer places for dust to accumulate.
- ☐ Use a HEPA filter in your vacuum.
- ☐ Let those piggies roam free. Remove shoes to leave the outdoors outside.
- ☐ Catch your idling habits. Turn off the car when waiting in parking lots or for busses.
- ☐ A clean home doesn't smell like synthetic scents. No need to spend your money here.

- ☐ Choose house paints with a zero or low VOC base.
- ☐ Choose fragrance-free products in the laundry room.
- ☐ Let indoor air out and outdoor air in.
- ☐ Purchase the biggest bag of baking soda you can find. Now, use it up as many ways as you can find.
- ☐ Give houseplants as gifts. Buy yourself one each time. Create your very own air cleansing army.
- ☐ Keep a bottle of vinegar in each bathroom. Pour. Sit. (The vinegar, not you.) Swish. Flush.
- ☐ Place homemade soft scrub in small containers near each sink or just baking soda with a little sponge for quick, shiny bathroom sinks.
- ☐ Replace your dishwashing rinse aid with vinegar (if you are using chlorine bleach free detergent).
- ☐ Pick your weeds. Or spray distilled white vinegar/lemon juice/castile soap cocktail onto weeds on a sunny day. Works wonders. Label the bottle "Mama's Secret Weed Killer" for an air of impressiveness.
- ☐ Need a fabric softener? You guessed it. A half cup of baking soda does the trick.
- ☐ Concerned about those really-important-to-disinfect areas? Find peace of mind through the fizzing of hydrogen peroxide. After cleaning with soap and hot water, sanitize with vinegar followed by a spray of hydrogen peroxide.

Teach everyone you cohabitate with why you are making these efforts, and share the responsibility.

For fifty more *Little Changes* tips, visit the Choose Wiser Website, and subscribe to the Be Choosy Newsletter.

Choose Wiser's Chemicals to Replace

The following chemicals are known carcinogens and/or endocrine disruptors or are harmful in other ways. While this isn't a complete list, these are the easiest to identify and replace around your home.

Ammonia
Glass cleaner, floor polish, drain cleaners, toilet cleaners, multi-surface cleaners, oven cleaners, stainless steel cleaners

Alkylphenol ethoxylates (APEs)
Detergents, cleaning products

Benzalkonium Chloride
Disinfecting hand soap, lotions

Benzene
Oven cleaner, detergent, auto product degreaser, adhesive remover, furniture polish, cigarette smoke, auto exhaust, gasoline, nail polish, nail polish remover

Bisphenol A (BPA)
Plastics (recycle symbol #7 may contain BPA), epoxy resin lining in food cans, some thermal receipt paper

Butylated hydroxytoulene (BHT)
Moisturizer, diaper rash ointment, mascara, lipstick, blush, shaving gel, frozen food, processed food (including but not limited to frozen pizza), cereal, and snack food

Chlorine Bleach
Laundry products, automatic dishwashing powder and liquid, toilet bowl cleaner

Coal Tars
Antidandruff shampoo, anti-itch/rash cream, pet shampoo

Di(2-ethylhexyl)phthalate (DEHP)
Plastic, cosmetics, household cleaners, fragrance ingredient

Formaldehyde
Nail polish, school glue, wood glue, laundry detergent, baby wash, hand soap, pet shampoo

Mineral Oils
Insect killer, furniture polish, fabric starch, hair conditioner, hair color, makeup remover, antiperspirant, deodorant, body wash, lotion, facial cream, hair remover, baby oil, diaper rash cream, toothpaste, nail polish, hair gel

Naphthalene
Carpet cleaner, toilet deodorizer, mothballs

Parabens
Creams, lotions, ointments

Petrolatum
Petroleum jelly, lipsticks, baby lotion, lotion, shaving cream, denture adhesive, diaper rash cream, antiperspirant, deodorant, hand cream, makeup remover

Perchloroethylene (PERC)
Degreaser, dry-cleaning fluid, tire shine, auto care product, stain and spot remover

Polyfluorinated chemicals (PFC)
Stain resistant coating for furniture, clothing and carpet, non-stick cookware

Propylene Glycol
Artificial food coloring, flavoring, medicine, hair color, moisturizers, conditioners

rBST
Milk, milk products

Styrene
Polystyrene (recycle code #6), disposable food trays, cups, egg cartons, carry out containers

Triclosan
Hand soap, toothpaste, mouthwash, dish liquid, body wash, face wash, deodorant, lip color, pet shampoo

Vinyl chloride (PVC)
Plastic (recycle code #3), tobacco smoke, food packaging, toys, cling wrap, vinyl shower curtains, cling wrap, plastic squeeze bottles, cooking oil

2, 4-Dichlorophenoxyacetic acid (2,4-D)
Household pesticide, weed control

To learn more about specific chemicals and products, explore:

Healthy Child, Healthy World: Chemical Profiles
http://healthychild.org

The Breast Cancer Fund: Chemical Glossary
http://www.breastcancerfund.org

EWG's Skin Deep Cosmetic Database
http://www.ewg.org/skindeep/

The Report on Carcinogens at National Toxicology Program,
Department of Health and Human Services
http://ntp.niehs.nih.gov

Household Products Database
U.S. Department of Health & Human Services
http://householdproducts.nlm.nih.gov/index.htm

Ways To Inspire Yourself and Others

- ☐ Send a gift wrapped *Little Changes* book to someone you care about.
- ☐ Use a 20% off *Little Changes* bulk discount for book clubs or groups.
- ☐ Invite Kristi Marsh to speak at your organization or community event.
- ☐ Or, Skype her to your book club.
- ☐ Subscribe to the Be Choosy Newsletter at:
  http://www.choosewiser.com/newsletter
- ☐ Subscribe to Choose Wiser's blog at:
  http://www.choosewiser.com/blog/
- ☐ Join discussions on Choose Wiser's Facebook page.
- ☐ Follow Choose Wiser on Twitter, @choosewiser.
- ☐ Visit the Choose Wiser website for information about Home Eco-Momics 101 resources.
- ☐ Email Choose Wiser to share your celebrations, ideas, and family traditions that educate children and teens about junky cosmetics, happy meat, genuine food, and nontoxic cleaning. Submissions may be shared in newsletters, blogs, or future writing.

Further Learning

Websites and Wallet Cards

10 Americans Video
http:/www.ewg.org/kidsafe

Beyond Pesticides
http:/beyondpesticides.org

Breast Cancer Fund
http:/www.breastcancerfund.org

Campaign for Safe Cosmetics
http:/www.safecosmetics.org

Center for Food Safety
http:/www.centerforfoodsaftey.org

Certified Humane®
http:/www.certifiedhumane.org

Eat Wild
http:/www.eatwild.com

Environmental Working Group's Shopper Guide to Pesticides in
Produce and Sunscreen Guide
http:/www.ewg.org

Good Guide
http:/www.goodguide.com

Green Cleaning Recipes
http:/www.womensvoices.org

Green Restaurant Association
http:/dinegreen.com

Healthy Child Health World
http://healthychild.org

Healthy Stuff
http:/www.healthystuff.org

Local Harvest
http:/www.localharvest.org

The Meatrix
http:/www.themeatrix.com

Non-GMO Shopping Guide
http:/www.responsibletechnology.org/buy-non-gmo

Organic Consumers Association
http:/www.organicconsumers.org

Recycling 101
http:/www.Earth911.org

Seafood Watch Program
http:/www.montereybayaquarium.org/cr/seafoodwatch.aspx

Skin Deep Cosmetic Database
http:/www.cosmeticsdatabase.com

Story of Stuff Video
http:/www.storyofstuff.com

Recommended Books and Films

New Dawn
Exposed: The Toxic Chemistry of Everyday Products and What's at Stake for American Power
Mark Schapiro. Chelsea Green Publishing, 2007

Our Stolen Future: Are We Threatening Our Fertility, Intelligence and Survival?
Theo Colborn, Dianne Dumanoski, and John Peterson Myers. Penguin Group, 1997

This Moment on Earth: Today's New Environmentalists and Their Vision for the Future
John Kerry, Teresa Heinz Kerry. Public Affairs, 2007

Silent Spring
Rachel Carson. Mariner Books, 2002

Smother
Not Just a Pretty Face: The Ugly Side of the Beauty Industry
Stacy Malkan. New Society Publishers, 2008

The Essential Green You! Volume Three.
Deirdre Imus. Simon & Schuster, 2008

Devour
American Wasteland.
Jonathan Bloom. Da Capo Press, 2010

Food, Inc. (movie)
http://takepart.com/foodinc

Bottomfeeder: How to Eat Ethically in a World of Vanishing Seafood
Taras Grescoe. Bloomsbury, 2008

Chew on This
Eric Schlosser, Charles Wilson. Houghton Mifflin, 2006

Food Matters: A Guide to Conscious Eating
Mark Bittman. Simon & Schuster, 2009

Food Rules: An Eater's Manual
Michael Pollan. The Penguin Group, 2009

Keep Chickens: Tending Small Flocks in Cities, Suburbs, and Other Small Spaces
Barbara Kilarski. Storey Publishing, 2003

The New American Diet: How secret "obesogens" are making us fat, and the 6-week plan that will flatten your belly for good!
Stephen Perrine with Heather Hurlock. Rodale, 2010

The Omnivore's Dilemma: The Secrets Behind What You Eat, Young Readers Edition
Michael Pollan. The Penguin Group, 2009

Seeds of Deception: Exposing Industry and Government Lies About the Safety of the Genetically Engineered Foods You're Eating
Jeffrey M. Smith. Yes! Books, 2003

The Unhealthy Truth: One Mother's Shocking Investigation into the Dangers of America's Food Supply-and What Every Family can Do to Protect Itself
Robyn O'Brien and Rachel Kranz. Broadway Books, 2009

Immerse
Green Clean: The Environmentally Sound Guide to Cleaning Your Home
Linda Mason Hunter, Mikki Halpin. DK Melcher Media, 2005

Healthy Child Healthy World: Creating a Cleaner, Greener, Safer Home
Christopher Gavigan. Dutton Adult, 2008

Slow Death by Rubber Duck: The Secret Danger of Everyday Things
Rick Smith, Bruce Lourie. Counterpoint, 2011

YOU: The Owner's Manual, Updated and Expanded Edition: An Insider's Guide to the Body that Will Make You Healthier and Younger
Mehmet C. Oz, Michael F. Roizen. William Morrow, 2008

Acknowledgements

I am deeply grateful....

- To Tanner, Kyle, and Kaytee; my Peace, Joy, and Love.
- To Ted, my rock and best friend.
- To my family. Mom, who taught me family is everything. Eric, my lil' bro, who inspires me to not just think about the world I live in but to passionately do my part.
- To Dad and Pam, who encourage me to live from my Inner Kiddie and who instilled in me the desire to cherish the body I was given.
- To those who support me unconditionally: Julie, Melanie, Natalie, and Cheleyne. Jenya. Allie. Peggy. Chuck and Hope. And Beth for teaching me early on that the Next Stop is always an Adventure.
- To my guardian Tara and my devoted friend Karen.
- To the creative genius and brilliant wit of my Queen Editor Rachel Vidoni. The world awaits your gifts!
- To my posse of women and my book club for fostering my voice, and to Rachel's book club for their invaluable comments.
- To Anna Nolan, Judy Bittner, and Lisa Galas for their invaluable comments and proofing that tightened this story.
- To my webmaster Douglas Heidland at DKM Studios, who is a perceptive visionary.
- To those who mentored me over a cup of tea, ceveche, or Thai lunch with thought provoking discussion: Stacy Malkan, Mia Davis, and Ted Schettler.

❧ To those who believed, listened, and invited me to share: Eileen Rappold of Personal Best Karate, Susan Finn of the Women's Business Network, Michelle Fitzgerald, Barbara Boone, Deb Balcarek, Maria Elena Police, Molly Vokey, Lori Prew, Amy Morse, Linda Publicover, Andrea Waldorf, and Lynn Loewald. Also, the nurses at Faulkner Hospital, the Easton Foodie Group, the Easton MOMS Club, Sue Bayley and Chris Kervian of Longmeadow High School, Alida Cantor of Langwater Farm, and Tri-County Toastmasters.

❧ To those who unknowingly changed my journey: Elizabeth Saunders, Cindy Luppi, Laura Sparks, Ann Black, Lori Voto, and Davis Baltz.

❧ To all those in Choose Wiser Facebook Nation whom I know only by tiny profile pictures and posts that remind me I am not alone.

❧ To Lindentree Farm: I am grateful for what you do for my family. We will never return to our old ways.

❧ To those whom I am honored to have interviewed and laughed with: Erin Boles, Robin Organ, Jessa Blades of Blades Natural Beauty, and Luke Penney of Leap Organics.

❧ To the "sheros" at the Campaign for Safe Cosmetics, Breast Cancer Fund, Women's Voices for the Earth, and Massachusetts Breast Cancer Fund. I am deeply grateful for the outreach and education you provide to the Everyday-Me's of the world.

❧ To those who saved me: Ellen McCarthy, Dr. Lawler, Dr. Parker, Dr. Morganstern, Michelle Ciszewski, Dr. Chun, Ellen LaCavita, and their compassionate support teams.

❧ *Most Especially,* ❧

To the mothers, fathers, sisters, brothers, and children I will never meet, who endured scourging chemotherapies and debilitating surgeries for the chance to wake another morning to live fully and lovingly.

About the Authors

Kristi Marsh

By day, Kristi is a flip-flop wearin', troop leadin', carpoolin', campin' kind of mom who is thrilled to watch her children blossom from one New England season to another. Given a spare moment, you might find her in a yoga pose in her backyard surrounded by hens, quizzing clerks in the grocery store (for fun), or learning how to cook an unfamiliar farm veggie. Regardless of what she's actually doing, she's always daydreaming about the next opportunity to pack up the kids for an afternoon on the beach, an evening around a campfire, or a cross-country road trip.

By evening, Kristi delights in donning heels and inspiring others in her Choose Wiser workshops where she inspires women to be self-advocates for their own environmental health. Her passion, humor, and presentations have been recognized by Prevention Magazine's Picture of Health, Clean Water Action's 2011 John O'Connor Award, Healthy Living Magazine's Champion of Health 2010 Awards, and Greenschool's 2009 Outstanding Leadership Award.

You can contact her at <u>kristimarsh@choosewiser.com</u>.

RachelVidoni

Rachel is currently a full-time freelance writer who loves to take meaty stories and turn them into delectable, mouthwatering (happy) hamburgers. Thanks to this project, she is now the proud owner of five laying hens, who reside in the most amazing chicken coop built by her initially-reticent-now-totally-on-board-husband. When she isn't editing books or writing, she grows fruits and veggies and makes a mean Blackberry Grand Marnier jam.

She is also a mediocre mom to three children who are pretty awesome despite her parenting gaffes. Rachel has published articles and essays in *The Boston Globe, Edible South Shore, Easton Journal, More.com, Easton Patch*, and she writes a bi-weekly parenting column at the *Good Enough Mother (GEM)* website. You can read more about her mediocre mom moves on her blog, www.eastcoastmusings.com. She guarantees you won't be a better parent after reading her stuff, but you will feel like one.

To read more of her writing or to inquire about a project, visit her website at www.rachelvidoni.com, or contact her at rgvidoni@hotmail.com.

Reader's Guide

In addition to the following discussion questions, I am available as a virtual guest at your book club via Skype. Inquire for availability at ChooseWiser.com.

1. If you were going to recreate your body starting next week, what current routines would you change?

2. Which topic in this Home Eco-Momics 101 smorgasbord did you connect with? GMOs? Endocrine disruptors? Personal care products? Household cleaners? Which subject was most jaw-dropping? Which ones were you already familiar with?

3. I shy away from categorizing myself with labels and struggle to name this lifestyle. To me, it's simply just about health. References elsewhere use "clean, holistic, green, nontoxic, eco-health, or environmental health." What associations do these words have? How would you describe this topic to a friend?

4. While presenting to audiences, I sense I am not teaching a new concept as much as I am awakening a "knowing" that already exists within many of my audience members. What is that innate knowledge?

5. I found reassurance and joy in the "aha" moment of, *We do learn*. Many followers like to recall "back in the day" stories. At one hospital presentation, nurses laughed at how they used to roll mercury from broken thermometers into balls. What behavior during your childhood would be thought of as reckless now?

6. Do you think reducing our abundant use of toxins is realistic? Why or why not? What feasible changes can you see happening in our culture in the next ten years?

7. Mia Davis from the Campaign for Safe Cosmetics reassured me I didn't have to be an expert to make an impact. I just had to be a caring human who wanted change. In our world of expert witnesses, quotes from doctors, scientific reports and constant news reporting, can a singular voice be impactful?

8. In an emotional moment, I broke down in the oncology office insisting I remain on the chemotherapy because I felt it would keep the cancer away, and I could go on being a mom. Have you ever been passionate (or possibly irrational) when standing up for something you felt strongly about? Discuss.

9. *"I might not understand why I'm drawn to this subject, but I have no doubt it's what I'm supposed to be doing."* Have you found your calling? Do we repress possible life callings because they may be eccentric or unusual?

10. A raw parenting moment brought me to question, *"When little souls outside the door hear, do you acknowledge or do you pretend? Do you reveal your private anguish and risks stealing bits of their innocence? Or push on without explanation, creating a silent divider, disconnecting those two souls?"* How much of your personal emotions do you share with your children? Is it better to hide and protect their innocence or share and discuss? Why?

11. The Breast Cancer Fund states that exposures to common environmental toxicants, including endocrine disrupting compounds, may be responsible in large part for the falling age of breast development in young girls. What mental and physical implications can you imagine happening as girls mature at younger ages?

12. During the development of *Little Changes*, the Safe Cosmetics Act, the Safe Chemicals Act, and a Toxic Chemicals Safety Act have been introduced into federal legislation. As a consumer, have you heard about these? What is it going to take to have legislation passed and implemented?

13. Some smaller, socially responsible brands are now owned by larger corporations that seemingly have a different eco-health positioning. Clorox owns Burt's Bees and Greenworks. Colgate owns Tom's of Maine. Dannon owns Stoneyfield Farm Yogurt. Is this a step forward? Does this make products affordable and accessible? Do you think this compromises the original integrity of the smaller brand? Do you think the parent company is trying to do better or just make a buck?

14. Where should the burden of proof lie when ensuring a product is safe? Is it the customer's responsibility? The government? The company selling the product? The manufacturer?

15. In our age of information, would you like *proof* of harm or wrongdoing before change is implemented? Or is the *threat* of harm, even if not fully established, enough cause for change? Would you keep the same viewpoint if you were a business owner? A parent? A politician?

16. Would your grocery list or food shopping routine change if genetically modified ingredients were labeled on your products? Why or why not?

17. *"When do we step back and challenge, is this really food at all?"* How crazy is it that we are pushed to define what food is? Imagine you are walking through a grocery store with a five year old. How would you describe what is food and what isn't? And if it isn't food, how would you explain what it's doing in the store? How do you define food?

18. What if, in twenty years, we discovered that cancer was caused by a bug bite or that allergies or obesity were easily explained by science that is currently undiscovered? Would your precautionary actions be for nothing?

19. Are you interested in continuing to learn with other women? What topic(s) would you like to learn more about first?

20. *"They were intelligent, caring, amazing women. I understand it's easier—choosing to remain unacquainted with the facts does make life simpler. Because once we know something, we can't not know it."* Who are the people in your life who would relish the message in this book? Who would be resistant to listening? Why? What would be a simple way to initiate conversation?

Notes

1. United States Environmental Protection Agency website, http://www.epa.gov/opp00001/factsheets/chemicals/deet.html.

2. United States Environmental Protection Agency website, http://www.epa.gov/pesticides/health/mosquitoes/pyrethroids4mosquitoes.htm.

3. United States Environmental Protection Agency website, http://www.epa.gov/oppsrrd1/REDs/factsheets/0002fact.pdf.

4. Carson, Rachel. *Silent Spring*. (New York: Mariner Books, 1990) 1.

5. Scholastic website, http://www2.scholastic.com/browse/article.jsp?id=4964.

6. United States Environmental Protection Agency website, http://www.epa.gov/aboutepa/history/topics/.

7. United States Environmental Protection Agency website, http://www.epa.gov/aboutepa/history/topics/.

8. United States Environmental Protection Agency website, http://www.epa.gov/aboutepa/history/topics/.

9. United States Environmental Protection Agency website, http://www.epa.gov/wastes/hazard/tsd/pcbs/.

10. Gray, Janet, Ph.D., *State of the Evidence:The Connection Between Breast Cancer And The Environment* (Breast Cancer Fund: Sixth Edition 2010).

11. WBUR On Point Radio website, *Our Toxic Environment*, http://onpoint.wbur.org/2007/10/29/our-toxic-environment.

12. Mark Schapiro, *Exposed: The Toxic Chemistry of Everyday Products And What's At Stake For American Power* (White River Junction: Chelsea Green Publishing, 2007), 10.

13. Schapiro, *Exposed: The Toxic Chemistry of Everyday Products And What's At Stake For American Power*, 11.

14. Schapiro, *Exposed: The Toxic Chemistry of Everyday Products And What's At Stake For American Power*, 24.

15. Cosmetic Ingredient Review website, http://www.cir-safety.org/.

16. Gray, *State of the Evidence*, 14.

17. Ibid., 16.

18. Ibid., 14.

19. Ibid., 14.

20. Philip Shabecoff, Alice Shabecoff, *Poisoned Profits: The Toxic Assault on Our Children* (New York: Random House, 2008), 39.

21. Gray, *State of the Evidence*, 13.

22. American Cancer Society, *Cancer Facts & Figures 2011*, 1.

23. Ibid.

24. Ibid.

25. Robyn O'Brien, *The Unhealthy Truth* (New York: Broadway, 2009).

26. Center for Disease Control and Prevention website, http://www.cdc.gov/vitalsigns/asthma/.

27. Center for Disease Control and Prevention website, http://www.cdc.gov/nchs/data/databriefs/db10.htm.

28. Moss BG, Yeaton WH (2011). *Young Children's Weight Trajectories and Associated Risk Factors: Results From the Early Childhood Longitudinal Study—Birth Cohort.* (American Journal of Health Promotion) 25 (3): 190–198.

29. Carson, *Silent Spring,* 48

30. National Institute Environmental Health Services – National Institute of Health website, http://www.niehs.nih.gov/about/materials/lead-fs.pdf.

31. National Geographic website, http://news.nationalgeographic.com/news/2010/05/100505-science-environment-ozone-hole-25-years.

32. Connecticut Department of Public Health website, http://www.ct.gov/dph/site/default.asp.

33. Fenton SE, *Endocrine-disrupting compounds and mammary gland development: Early exposure and later life consequences.* Endocrinology, 147:S18-S24, 2006.

34. Breast Cancer Fund, *State of the Evidence: The Connection between Breast Cancer and the Environment.* 12 .

35. Environmental Working Group website, http://www.ewg.org/chemindex/chemicals/22794.

36. United States Food and Drug Administration, http://www.fda.gov/Cosmetics/ProductandIngredientSafety/ProductInformation/ucm137224.htm#analyses.

37. Carson, *Silent Spring.* Xv.

38. National Public Radio website, Allison Aubrey, *When it Comes to Shampoo, Less is More,* www.npr.org.

39. Food and Drug Administration website, http://www.fda.gov/Cosmetics/GuidanceComplianceRegulatoryInformation/ucm074162.htm.

40. Women's Voices for the Earth website, http://womenandenvironment.org.

41. Environmental Working Group website, http://www.ewg.org/skindeep/faq/.

42. Gray, *State of the Evidence,* 44.

43. Center for Disease Control website, *U.S. Center for Disease Control's 2005 National Report on Human Exposure to Environmental Chemicals,* www.cdc.gov.

44. Michael Pollan, *The Omnivore's Dilemma: A Natural History of Four Meals* (New York: Penguin, 2006), 1.

45. Michael Pollan website, *Farmer in Chief," Michael Pollan, The New York Times Magazine,* http://michaelpollan.com/articles-archive/farmer-in-chief/.

46. United States Environmental Protection Agency website, http://epa.gov/opp00001/about/index.htm.

47. National Cancer Institute website, *Environmental Factors in Cancer: Reducing Environmental Cancer Risk, What We Can Do Now,* http://deainfo.nci.nih.gov/advisory/pcp/annualReports/index.htm.

48. United States Environmental Protection Agency website, http://www.epa.gov/pesticides/factsheets/securty.htm.

49. Beyond Pesticides website, http://www.beyondpesticides.org/health/alzheimers.htm.

50. Pediatrics: Official Journal of the American Academy of Pediatrics website, http://pediatrics.aappublications.org/content/early/2010/05/17/peds.2009-3058.abstract.

51. Gray, *State of the Evidence,* 72.

52. Environmental Working Group FoodNews website, http://www.foodnews.org/reduce.php.

53. California Department of Pesticide Regulation website, http://www.cdpr.ca.gov/docs/emon/pubs/fatememo/carbofuran.pdf.

54. The Daily Green Website, *EPA to Ban Carbofuran Pesticide Residue on Food,* Dan Shapely, http://green.yahoo.com/blog/daily_green_news/61/epa-to-ban-carbofuran-pesticide-residue-on-food.html.

55. How Stuff Works website, *Should we be worried about the dead zone in the Gulf of Mexico? ,* Jacob Silverman, http://science.howstuffworks.com/environmental/earth/oceanography/dead-zone.htm 04 October 2011.

56. BBC News website, http://news.bbc.co.uk/2/hi/science/nature/6904249.stm.

57. Slate Magazine, http://www.slate.com/id/2083482/.

58. Earthjustice website, www.earthjustice.org/gmo.

59. Environmental Health Perspectives website, http://ehp03.niehs.nih.gov.

60. World Farm Animal Day website, http://www.wfad.org/statistics.

61. American Grass Fed Beef website, www.americangrassfedbeef.com/faq-grass-fed-beef.asp.

62. Take Part website, http://www.takepart.com/article/2011/11/04/antibiotics-animal-production-increased-2010.

63. Los Angeles Times website, http://www.latimes.com/health/boostershots/drugs/la-heb-antibiotics-121410,0,4660198.story.

64. Stephen Perrine, *The New American Diet* (New York:Rodale,2010), 12.

65. Perrine, *The New American Diet*, 12.

66. Pollan, *The Omnivore's Dilemma: A Natural History of Four Meals, 333.*

67. Mother Earth News website, http://www.motherearthnews.com/Real-Food/2007-10-01/Tests-Reveal-Healthier-Eggs.aspx.

68. Institute for Responsible Technology website, http://responsibletechnology.org/gmo-dangers/gm-hormones-in-dairy .

69. Gray, *State of the Evidence, 72.*

70. Gray, *State of the Evidence, 75.*

71. Perrine, *The New American Diet, 94.*

72. USDA website, *Agriculture Fact Book*, http://www.usda.gov/factbook/chapter2.htm.

73. Jonathon Bloom, *American Wasteland: How America Throws Away Nearly Half of Its Food (and What We Can Do About It),* (Cambridge: Da Capo Press

74. Fast Food Marking website, *Fast Food F.A.C.T.S.: Food Advertising to Children and Teens Score,* http://www.fastfoodmarketing.org/media/FastFoodFACTS_Report.pdf.

75. Gray, *State of the Evidence, 42.*

76. Rick Smith, Bruce Lourie, *Slow Death by Rubber Duck*, (Berkeley: Counterpoint, 2009), 228.

77. Alliance for Healthy Tomorrow website, www.healthytomorrow.org .

78. New York Times website, *New Alarm Bells About Chemicals and Cancer*, Nicholas D. Kristof, http://www.nytimes.com/2010/05/06/opinion/06kristof.html.

79. Carson, *Silent Spring*, 68.

Notes and Ideas

LITTLE CHANGES

40577222R00136

Made in the USA
Lexington, KY
10 April 2015